D0396248

A Lotus Flower
In Muddy Waters

Stuart Perrin

CCCF Religious Services Book
Personal Property

Crosby-Blakeway #13681159
Name   SID

BLUE KITE PRESS

Second Edition Copyright © by Stuart Perrin 2014
stuartperrin.com

Originally published under the title *A Deeper Surrender: notes on a spiritual life* in 2001 by Hampton Roads Publishing Co.

All rights reserved. No part of this book may be used or reproduced in any manner whatsoever without written permission except for brief passages in connection to a review.

Cover design: Winnie Chaffee, Tim Chi Ly, Robert Sink

Cover photos: Winnie Chaffee

Library of Congress Control Number: 2014908900
North Charleston, SC

Perrin, Stuart, 1942 -
A Lotus Flower In Muddy Waters / by Stuart Perrin — 2nd ed
      p. cm.
ISBN: 978-1499508758
1. Perrin, Stuart — Meditation, Yoga, Spirituality, Self-Help
2. Author, American

A Lotus Flower In Muddy Waters by Stuart Perrin
© 2014 ebook—1st edition

Other Books by Stuart Perrin

Little Sisters

Rudi: The Final Moments

Moving On: Finding Happiness in a Changed World

A Deeper Surrender: Notes on a Spiritual Life

Leah: A Story of Meditation and Healing

The Mystical Ferryboat

Dedication

To Rudi,

Without whose love, guidance,
and profound spiritual teachings,
I could never have risen to the surface of muddy waters.

To my daughter, Ania Devi Perrin, who lives
and will always live in the center of my heart.

Acknowledgments

Robert Sink for a wonderful interior and cover design for this book; Winnie Chaffee for the beautiful photo of a lotus flower; Michael Wombacher for transcribing the book; Hampton Roads for the original publication; Kristina Jones for her constant support in all my efforts; Alice Stipak for a great job of scanning the original book and Anne Kohlstaedt for her support; Paula Pennant because she found an original copy of the book in a musty London bookshop and became a close friend; and all the incredible people who read the original book, contacted me, and told me how much it helped them in their lives.

Preface

This timeless book, *A Lotus Flower in Muddy Waters* by Stuart Perrin, is one of the most important, revelatory, and generously written studies of its kind in contemporary spiritual literature — a twentieth century guidebook for actualizing one's inner life. It explores the practice of Kundalini Yoga's therapeutic, spiritual and esoteric applications and is as relevant to modern day seekers as Sri Swami Yogananda's *Autobiography of a Yogi* was to those who read it in the twentieth-first century.

Author and teacher, Stuart Perrin, was born in New York City. As a child, he exhibited unusual spiritual gifts and sought to learn and understand the deepest teachings of eastern and western religions. After years of domestic and international travel in search of a guru, Mr. Perrin returned to his home in New York where he met Rudi (Swami Rudrananda). Thus began his initiation into what would become a lifetime of personal growth that culminated in mastery of Kundalini Yoga and the ability to pass on teachings, techniques and benefits of the spiritual practice he originally learned from Rudi.

A Lotus Flower in Muddy Waters shares with the reader profound and ageless teachings. The following quotes from the book (just a small sample) show the relevance of Mr. Perrin's insights into contemporary life: "Within every person there's a voice that guides him or her to higher levels of consciousness, a voice that speaks from the heart. We have to learn to trust it. It's our teacher;" or, "The less ego we have cluttering up our inner lives, the more room there is for spiritual energy, but people cling to anxiety and neurosis out of familiarity. They'd rather be crazy than be nothing... it takes guts to surrender to the unknown;" or, "It's easy to keep one's heart open when good times are here, but nobility of soul is found in people who keep their hearts open during bad times as well... Can we find love, joy, sweetness, and gratitude in the dark night of the human soul? That's a true test of our connection with God." Mr. Perrin gives us a clear and practical understanding of how one can live a happy life in a confused and crazy world. A perennial storyteller, he uses uncomplicated language to share his personal experiences on the spiritual path.

I first met Stuart Perrin in the fall of 1980. I had been looking for a spiritual teacher for most of my life and had tried many forms of meditation. Through the ensuing years, I've marveled at the impact of that first meeting. Time and reality changed in a profound manner, and it was apparent that I had found my teacher and the person who would most deeply affect my life. The training that I've received from Stuart has enriched me and has paved the way, as I believe it will pave the reader's way, to a happy and dynamic inner life. In contemporary terms, Stuart is the one teacher I have met who *walks the talk*. Please. Do yourself a favor! Read this book!

Kristina Jones
May, 2014

Author's Note

When a book helps people to re-examine themselves and find clear insight and motivation to live more creative lives, it has to stay in print. Originally published as *A Deeper Surrender: Notes on a Spiritual Life,* I decided to change the title to a more befitting, *A Lotus Flower in Muddy Waters*. It struck me that every human being is like a lotus flower, every human being lives in muddy waters and has to find a connection to light and love and happiness in their lives. We weren't born here to be miserable. Infants are sweet and cuddly and radiate joy. It's a pleasure to hold them, to play with them, to allow their sweetness to be part of our lives. Somewhere along the way, that cuddliness disappears and we're conditioned to believe that struggle and unhappiness is all life has to offer. It's not true. Every one of us was born here to have a wonderful life. We just have to transform our suffering into love, our fear into joy, and develop inside ourselves the security to live with an open heart.

The seed of a lotus flower is buried in the mud, but the flower itself opens on a lake and greets the sun. We too can greet the sun; we too can be happy. We just have to learn how. One line in the book has always stayed with me: "The only successful people on earth are happy people." What separates a happy person from an unhappy person is an open heart; and the heart, delicate and quite beautiful, is also like a flower that needs a seed, roots and a means of receiving nourishment. *A Lotus Flower in Muddy Waters* speaks to this quandary. It guides readers to a place within themselves where it's possible to live a less tense, calmer and more fulfilling life.

Stuart Perrin
May 8, 2014

Contents

Introduction

In my youth I read about great sages who lived in swamps and deserts and caves and devoted every moment of their lives to God. Many profound spiritual books were written by men in the ancient Middle East, in classical Greece, and in century's old Tibetan and Indian monasteries. In today's world, where most of the population of earth is centered in cities, where we have to defend ourselves against the nonstop blare of cars and trucks and ambulances and fire engines, where street and pedestrian traffic don't allow us a moment of inner peace, where money and power drown out the need for spirituality and a cast of urban characters promotes itself in whatever costume suits its needs, where to deaden the "slings and arrows" of stress after a day's work we consume straight-up double martinis at Happy Hour in bars frequented by equally stressed out seekers after fame and fortune. In today's world, it's almost impossible for us to believe that a city dweller can have a spiritual life. At the same time, we are all human beings, and our basic needs, though they manifest differently, are very much the same as people who lived in antiquity. What do we really want: to love and be loved, to be happy, to find a real purpose for our existence? Having interacted with thousands of people across the globe, it became clear to me that it's more difficult to find a happy person than to uncover the secrets of the Holy Grail. Rarely have I met anyone who doesn't want to be happy. People have told me that it is impossible to be happy, that it is a fool's quest — the condition of the human race is to suffer without any rhyme or reason, and sometimes, the chaos of city life can force one to almost accept this as truth.

What is most astonishing in this little book is that the words written come from a person who was raised on the streets of the South Bronx — a person born in a Bronx hospital, not in a manger surrounded by wise men and kings, a person who didn't emerge from a lotus flower in the Himalayan hinterlands. My parents knew nothing about ancient Hindu and Buddhist meditation practices. They were steeped in the idea of being Jewish — not religious Jews, but more of a tribal sense of belonging to a group of people that had the same heritage and represented a safe and familiar way of living. This tribal mentality hasn't disappeared from the earth. People still seek out racial and religious similarities in other people, bond with them, and feel a false sense of security that stems from skin color and common religious beliefs. To a certain degree, the compressed lifestyle of city dwellers can create a color blindness that is very healthy. I see it in my daughter whose friends are a wonderful blend of every race and religion. When a person has evolved within himself or herself to where they are living a spiritual life, religion disappears, race disappears, and they live according to a higher truth: everything around them is God's creation. They don't need ritual or dogma to be enlightened; they don't need priests, rabbis or gurus. They are the children of God living in the light of God, and life itself has become their teacher. When we're open enough to listen to what life has to teach, we can tap its fountain of wisdom and transform it into a compassionate means of interacting with other human beings.

Though this book talks extensively about meditation and the need to develop a chakra system that's strong enough to connect us to spirit, I'd like to clarify something: because one meditates it doesn't necessarily mean they are having a spiritual life. Meditation is simply a tool to be used to open the chakra system. A spiritual life is a whole different thing. It goes on twenty-four/seven. It takes place in the temple, on the street, at work, at home with our families — wherever life takes us and whatever interaction we have with the world. Once we manage to sustain an open chakra system, the universe will provide us with knowledge, wisdom, detachment, and the ability to live compassionate lives. Meditation is a non-sectarian tool that helps us to develop the highest levels of our humanity.

There are certain truths that have never changed. The need to be happy is one of them and that need is often hidden in the recesses of human confusion. I've come to realize that happy people are enlightened people. It's no more complicated than that. If you find a person (atheist, agnostic, religious or otherwise) that lives with their heart open and gives and receives unconditionally, you'll find a person who is living a spiritual life. You'll also find a person who has learned everything there is to learn about life on earth. Some cynics might say that this is naïve or innocent, but, when the heart is closed, there's almost always a deadness in people's eyes — a lack of trust that keeps them from loving one another and forces them to communicate on a level that resembles sharks trying to devour smaller fish for lunch. If we are filled with the chaos of mind and emotion, there's no room for wisdom, and without wisdom, compassion will never find its place in the world.

The original title of this book was *A Spiritual Life*. When the editor at Hampton Roads first read my manuscript twelve years ago, he told me that the title wasn't commercial enough. He suggested: *A Deeper Surrender: Notes on a Spiritual Life*. I agreed, mostly because I didn't want to rock the boat. Finding a publisher was, and still is, a very difficult undertaking in today's world. It was only after the book was published that I discovered most people associate the word "surrender" with "giving up." In a deeper sense, surrender means letting go, making room — the realization that if we're full of ourselves, there's no room for spirit to come in. So I decided, in republishing this book, to opt for *A Lotus Flower In Muddy Waters* — a simple and poetic title to a book that guides the reader over a path taken by a kid who grew up on the streets of the South Bronx and discovered that God lives in New York City and in every corner of the globe.

CHAPTER ONE:

The Birth Of A Spiritual Teacher

Q: Could you tell us about your background, where you were brought up, what you did as a young adult, and some of the early influences in your life?

I was born and raised in a lower middle-class Jewish family in the South Bronx—a very important factor in my life, because, as a child, I felt a restless need to expand to new horizons. Being raised in the Bronx brought a certain street-smart wisdom that I still use today, a language that helps me to distinguish between things real and things not real. I was a very solitary person. Though I had many friends and played sports, I never shared my deepest thoughts and feelings with other people. Not satisfied with banal answers to profound questions, seeing great pain and deep unhappiness everywhere, I withdrew into myself. I listened to an inner voice speak about God and higher creative energy in the universe.

Q: Did you feel that there was much more to life than what you were experiencing?

Yes. As I got older, it got worse. I became more and more alienated. I spent weeks and months by myself in a world of thoughts, dreams, and visions in a transcendental world that took me away from practical things—that isolated me even further from people in my life.

Q: What did your father do?

My father worked in the garment center as a cutter of patterns. He'd work eight to ten hours a day, come home, eat, watch TV, play cards, and rarely, if ever, did he show interest in theatre, music, painting, or anything related to the arts. He enjoyed a good boxing match, baseball or basketball game, a pastrami sandwich, and chicken soup. A man of basics, he loved and supported his family to the best of his ability. He died when I was sixteen, a death that kick-started my spiritual quest.

Racked by fever, shaking and incoherent, foaming at the mouth, unconscious and coma-like for days on end, my father didn't recognize my mother, sister, or me. The will to live petered out of him. A few hours before he died, the fever went away and his deep brown eyes had a sparkle of light in them. I sat near his bed, took his hand, and asked him if he recognized me. He shook his head and whispered, "Yes." The room filled up with light. I experienced a spiritual awakening and a sense of peace I'd never known before. I saw God in my father's eyes, a divine energy that radiated light, love, forgiveness, and total surrender. He died three hours later.

Shaken by the experience, I reevaluated my life purpose. My interest in sports waned. I latched on to Bohemian lifestyles and the beatnik thing going on full blast at the time. I read books on Eastern religions, on existentialism, then the poems of Rilke, Rimbaud, Baudelaire, Whitman, Ginsberg, and, more than anything else, I wanted to leave my neighborhood and get out of my family's house.

Q: Would you say you had an inclination to seek some form of enlightenment in this life?

Definitely. I wrote visionary poetry, meditated, studied hatha yoga, and struggled day and night with my demon mind. My introversion forced me to look out at a dark world, a surreal world, a world full of illusion, a world that circled my inner being. I couldn't free myself from an overactive mind that conjured up strange images of life and myself.

Q: You couldn't get past your mind? What does that mean? How serious a problem is it to not get past one's mind?

It's the number one problem all human beings face. The human mind is noisy, tense, righteous, anxiety-ridden, chaotic and diffi-cult to deal with. It's also the most powerful instrument we have. People rarely, if ever, use the energy of the mind in a beneficial way.

Q: As a product of the 1950s and 1960s, were you influenced by writers such as Jean-Paul Sartre, Albert Camus, and Jack Kerouac?

I read most of Sartre, Camus, and Kafka, not so much Kerouac, except On the Road. Existentialist writers influenced my thought process, playwrights like Samuel Beckett and Eugene Ionesco; their absurdist ideas forced me to grapple with day-to-day reality. The concept of nothingness loomed above me like a psychedelic sky in a Munch painting, me and an army of shadows at odds with each other, the mad and the not-so-mad boldly walking together in fantastic landscapes, the thought that one day I'd no longer be alive, I'd no longer exist, life would continue without me. Why come to a place that lacks permanence? Why set up shop in a transient world? Death made everything around me absurd, death and its blunt perspective of terminable landscapes where every path leads to nothingness, every activity imbues itself with absurdity. "There must be something without limitation," I used to say to myself, "something transcendental, something more important than full speed dashes of neurotic impulse that crashes into brick walls."

Absurdity drove me to a spiritual life. It forced me to look in places my family and friends dared not enter, in places where rational, well-worked-out theorems of man's existence on Earth were shredded by infinite energy in the universe, by God who created reality from particles of dust. I saw a world without lim-itation, a world that transcended thought, mind, emotion, matter, money, power, almost every goal coveted by the human race. A new logic presented itself to me, one that pierced the veil of illu-sion, one that allowed me to make choices, to no longer torment myself, to laugh at the absurd, and to no longer fear death. It made sense of even senseless things. It gave me the ability to live quietly in a stress-filled world.

Q: How did you transform your life?

I found a spiritual teacher.
My father died when I was sixteen. He left me one great legacy—three hours of quiet introspection and surrender in a hospital room filled with light, peace, and inner glow. The last three hours of his life were a miracle. I wondered why he waited forty-nine years to find inner peace, why it happened three hours before his death?

Even at a young age, I realized it would be impossible to find God by my lonesome. I needed a teacher, someone who'd been over the path, who fought the demon mind and emotions, who survived his own craziness. I traveled to Europe and North Africa. I studied the Vedas, the Bhagavad-Gita, the Old and New Testaments, books on Zen, Islam, Christianity, mythology, literature, and poetry. I'd smoke a joint and read the Old Testament, hallucinate, and see Kabbalistic diagrams of the universe. Later on, I read about Kabbalah, about the Sephirotic Tree, numerology, mystical paths to God, the book beneath the book in the Old Testament. It all made sense to me. It forced me to go even deeper within myself, to try to center and balance myself, but I lacked discipline. I saw confusion both inside and outside myself. The texts I read, though they made perfect sense, did nothing more than tease me. They revealed profound mystical secrets but were as silent as the dead when asked how to integrate these secrets into my life.

Q: Did you feel hopeless about everything?

Numb, hopeless, cut off, frightened, but willing to struggle with myself, willing to look for answers, willing to make a conscious effort to find a spiritual teacher. My insecurity made me more determined. I couldn't stand living in fear; I couldn't stand the pain in my heart, the ache in my gut, the noise rattling my brain. I had no interest in saving the world. Even at an early age, I realized messianic kingdoms were God's problem, not mine. First, I had to figure out how to survive my own day, and then I could worry about helping other people.

I sat with swamis and rishis and yogis and rebbes and gurus of every shape, size, form, and background. I meditated and chanted and read sacred texts, but never, not for a moment, did these teachers touch the core of my being. I took LSD, DMT, smoked grass until my ears were like chimneys, but nothing revealed how to quiet the mind, touch God, stay in permanent contact with higher energy in the universe. Learning made it worse. To know something does not mean you live what you know. There's a void between mind and action. If there's hell on Earth, it's got to be aberrated knowledge not rooted to practical living.

I rode the psychedelic roller coaster for nine years. At age twenty-five, I found myself in a Spanish jail. Miserable and ready to kill myself, I had reached bottom. Drugs were not the answer, and the gurus I'd met did little or nothing for my inner life. I asked for God's help. I knew if something didn't change, I'd soon be dead or living in a sanatorium. I read and reread the Bhagavad-Gita in my cell. I prayed, meditated, and asked over and over again for answers. The bottom's no fun. Its only benefit is you can't get much lower. The only way out is up.

Three weeks after getting out of jail, I met a spiritual teacher in New York named Rudi.

Q: Can you tell us how you met Rudi (Swami Rudrananda), who played such an important role in your life?

After being released from prison, after bending down and kissing the Earth and thanking God for my freedom, I returned to Paris, telephoned my friend Charlie in the States, and asked him to send me a plane ticket to New York. A week later, a ticket arrived. I went back to New York. I lived with this same friend in a tenement apartment on 21st Street in Manhattan, a railroad flat with bathtub in the kitchen and toilet in the public hallway. I slept on the floor and survived because of his generosity. I had no job, no money, no prospects for a job—nothing but a broken spirit and a great deal of confusion.

One evening, at about five o'clock, Charlie and I went to eat at a Middle Eastern restaurant on Seventh Avenue. It was a beautiful evening, mild, springlike, with a gentle breeze and a clear sky, so we decided to walk to the restaurant. First we walked south on Eighth Avenue, then east on Greenwich Street, then south on Seventh Avenue. We passed an Oriental art and antique shop and looked in the window. My friend said to me, "You like this stuff. Why don't we go in?" All my life I'd been interested in Asian art, religion, philosophy, food.

"I'm broke," I said. "I don't have any money. What am I going to do in there?"

"It doesn't cost to look," Charlie said.

"Then let's go in."

We walked into the store, a tiny store as I remember it, but a store packed with Asian artifacts. At its center, a five-foot, eight-inch balding, heavyset man who wore an orange tee shirt and beige chino pants and sandals stood by himself and watched a few browsers. I walked up to him. I don't know why, but his presence drew me like a magnet. "I'm Rudi," he said. His eyes sparkled, and rays of light emanated from his body. For a moment, everything in the store disappeared as if I'd just smoked grass or hash or something. "My God," I said to myself. "What's going on?" He showed me a photo of himself lying on the floor in an ecstatic, trance-like position with his teacher's picture superimposed in his heart and a swami sitting next to him on a chair.

"If you want to study with me, come here tomorrow night at five o'clock," he said.

"Okay," I heard myself say. "I'll be here."

As I walked out of the store, I turned to Rudi. He smiled at me, a smile so full of love, so beautiful, it went directly into my heart. I saw a halo of light that surrounded his body, the same light I'd seen in the hospital room the day my father died—an ethereal light, a divine emanation.

After dinner, Charlie and I went back to his apartment. On the stairwell, we met a mutual friend, a man who'd lived in the tenement building for twenty-some-odd years. "How would you like to have some tea?" He asked us. "In my apartment."

"Okay," Charlie said. We followed him into his apartment. There we found, in a thirty-eight-dollar-a-month railroad flat, an Oriental art collection worth hundreds of thousands of dollars.

"Where did you get this stuff?" I asked.

"There's a guy in Greenwich Village named Rudi. He has a

shop. I bought most of it from him."

Shivers went up and down my spine. The gods are talking to me, I thought. I'd better listen.

As we left our neighbor's apartment, a place neither of us had visited before, I said to Charlie, "I've got to see the man I met in the Oriental art shop. Something happened today. Something extraordinary happened to me today."

At five o'clock the following afternoon, I went to Rudi's store. He welcomed me with a big hug, showed me a meditation exercise, and from that moment we were inseparable—guru-disciple, father-son, call it what you want, but a relationship that set me on a path to God. He taught me what I thirsted for; he showed me how to get past myself.

A year later, I asked him, "What happened the day we met?"

"I saw you looking in the window of my store," he said. "It was like seeing my son lost in the universe. I pulled you in the door."

That's how I met Rudi. It took nine years of looking to find him. I walked past his shop hundreds of times before I went in, a walk I regularly took to Greenwich Village. "You've spent all these years listening to yourself," I thought after I met him. "Look what's happened. Now you have to listen to someone else."

Studying with Rudi was a real kick. All my preconceptions broke down. The apples and maple-syrup sugarcoated image of guru disappeared in a flash. He was the most sacrilegious person I'd ever met; at the same time, the most spiritual, iconoclastic, loving, irreverent seeker after truth God put on Earth. He disliked institutions, foundations, houses of worship, structured situations that shoved dogma down the throats of trusting congregations, dogma that controlled people instead of freeing them. He forced me to live in a constant state of surrender. All ideas of God and spirituality had to be tossed in the garbage, and I mean everything.

The first time he invited me to his apartment, I sat cross-legged at his feet, thrilled to be with my teacher— perhaps, I thought, the most powerful spiritual being I'd ever met. Rudi sat in half-lotus on a leather armchair. He asked one of his students to bring him a Scotch and water. I had my own ideas of purity, God, right-living on Earth, alcohol, smoking, vegetarianism, and holier-than-thou thoughts about the spiritual path.

You could get up and walk out, I thought, while saying to myself, "How can Rudi be my guru? My guru can't drink Scotch and water while I sit at his feet meditating." I had to surrender. My thoughts went on and on like this until my heart opened, I relaxed, and realized it's not for me to judge anyone on Earth. It is only for me to surrender.

It was the first and last time I'd ever see Rudi drink alcohol.

"The act of surrender gets you closer to God," he said to me when I first met him. "A guru defies preconception. He breaks down barriers that separate spiritual seekers from enlightenment until all that's left is nothingness, all that's left is a connection with God. If anyone ever asks you what is the 'guru', tell them 'life.' Its myriad manifestations are the greatest teacher of all.

"At best, I'm the servant of God," he went on, "and the servant of my students. If I forget this, I'm unworthy of the orange robe I wear. I shouldn't be a teacher."

"The guru reflects the disciple's limitations. You love him, you hate him, you don't know what to do with him, but, in time, you discover, it's not the guru you dislike, but yourself—your own fear, anger, insecurity, boorishness, stupidity, and ignorance. You're not angry at the guru; you're angry at your inability to get to the other side of your insane self, at your inability to free yourself from yourself and get closer to spiritual enlightenment. The guru forces you to deepen your inner life. That's hard to take. It means you have to surrender; it means you've got to grind the ego into particles of dust."

I was with Rudi when he died in an airplane crash. I held his hand, loved him, and considered it a great blessing to be with him the moment he died. He taught me that the guru doesn't die; he lives in the disciple's heart. His physical presence serves one purpose: to kick disciples in the ass and make them work harder on themselves. After we hit the mountain and I realized he was dead, I heard a voice speak inside me, "Now you'll find out whether you got any training," it said. "Now you'll discover what the last six years were about."

"I no longer have a life," I said to myself. "I no longer am Stuart, not the Stuart who existed prior to the crash. I'm nothing now but a servant of God. You don't walk away from an airplane crash and think you still have a life. The reason I'm alive is Rudi. Before he died, he put his life into me."

I'd walk with him through the streets of New York as if he were an immutable life force, never once did I believe anything could hurt him or kill him. I'd often think, no problem to protect him, no problem to hurl my body in the face of danger. But Rudi was always one step ahead of me. When the moment of truth presented itself, he put his life in me. I didn't die and put my life in him.

Q: Could you tell us a little more about Rudi?

Born in East New York, a rough section of Brooklyn, Rudi's psychic gifts became apparent to him at an early age. High Tibetan lamas visited him in dreams and visions. He could read palms, see auras, and look prophetically into people's futures. In his twenties, he used these gifts to develop a meditation practice that unified ancient Hindu and Buddhist teachings with Gurdjieff, Pak Subud, bagels and lox, practical living, and innate understanding that breath and mind were tools to develop the chakras that linked him directly to higher energy in the universe. It was a meditation technique indigenous to Western living, a work strong enough to grind up tension, to transform day-to-day pressure into positive energy. The Earth's a Pandora's box replete with pressure and tension. It's fostered billion dollar drug firms that administer uppers and downers, inners and outers, pills and more pills to keep people calm. "If you learn to breathe properly," Rudi once said to me, "and to use the mind properly, you can transform the craziness of modern day life into spirituality. It's less expensive than drugs, doctors, and therapy. The only hitch is it takes a lot of work."

Rudi's sense of humor lit up hundreds of dark situations. He made light of human soap operas, obstacles, fears, and insecurities; always cheek-in-jowl, he made me understand drama's a substitute for an inner life. A person full of God's energy has little or no time for emotional boxing matches. He doesn't play games. He respects other people. "Less is more," Rudi must have said a thousand times.

He dealt successfully in Oriental art and antiques, and was perhaps the first dealer in the West to sell Hindu/Buddhist art on a large scale. His store was part-temple, part-emporium, a place where meditation students gathered, curators visited, collectors browsed, and dealers bargained, a mishmash of comings and goings. He loved being at the center of it all; he loved the constant play of life around him.

He also loved food. The breakfast table overflowed with bagels, lox, cream cheese, assorted meats and cereals, a smorgasbord of tastes for a huge palette, food to be shared with people close to him; a Jewish mama, a big tit, and a juicy vehicle for God's energy on Earth. He took a big bite out of life. I remember him comparing life to a smorgasbord. "I want to eat from every corner of the table," he said. "I want there to be nothing to come back for."

I spent years looking for a teacher capable of living what he taught. Most gurus I'd met preached the time-worn "love, peace, and eat vegetables" mantra, then retreated to boring, mundane, and mediocre existences. Rudi could take a bite out of life. He lived in the moment. He spontaneously channeled higher energy into joyous, intense, conscious, God-serving, and egoless living. His material success in no way interfered with his spiritual practice. He saw no separation between the two. One nurtured the other. At the same time, neither controlled him. He had a sense of humor about things. "We're born to be happy," he'd say. "Every human being should have a wonderful life; every human being should cherish freedom." But you don't get free by cowering in darkness. You get free by exposing yourself to life, by letting life be your teacher, by expanding your capacity as a human being. It's to have and be free of what you have, to live without fear, to come out of the darkness. No one's ever free of money until they've had money; no one's ever free of relationships until they've had them. The rest is a state of mind.

Many people on the spiritual path say, "I don't need money, I don't need relationships. To have a spiritual life, I've got to be celibate, I've got to be a vegetarian, I've got to be this, and I've got to be that." Yet they crave the exact opposite. They waste their time day-dreaming about sex, wealth, position, power, or hide from their true nature in a holier-than-thou cocoon, afraid to come out, afraid to experience life's multifaceted ways. The two most dangerous things in life are purity and promiscuity. The former is a self-righteous, starched, and insane state that traps people in well-insulated bubbles; the latter is creative energy without discipline. I've never met a pure person. I've met holy rollers that preach the gospel of purity with their hands in your pocket, with soft sounding and smooth words that rankle with the promise of God, words that sugarcoat hollow truths and make congregations feel guilty. I've met Hindu, Jewish, Buddhist, and Christian holy rollers caught in their own images of God. Preaching gospel according to their own interpretations of scripture, they separate life into half-baked truisms that siphon humanity's essential fluids. They take the bagels, lox, and cream cheese out of living.

Most poor people are trapped by poverty, and most rich people are trapped by wealth. Very few people, rich or poor, are happy. I've rarely, if ever, met a person free of himself. Rudi fought his way out of the slums of Brooklyn. He built a small financial empire, but he never forgot his connection with God. His capacity to give, to share, to use his success for spiritual purposes; to never, not for a moment, believe he was anything but a vehicle for higher energy, inspired me. His capacity to live in the world and outside the world at the same time, to transform tension into creativity, and to share that creativity with those he loved, inspired me to learn from him. He taught me that spiritual work cannot be defined.

Q: *How long were you with Rudi?*

Six years. Many hours were spent sitting at his feet, drawing *shakti* from him, listening to him talk about his life and working to develop my own spiritual connection to God. *Shakti* is spiritual energy that emanates from a guru and nurtures the inner life of his or her disciples. He made it clear to me how little I understood and how far I had to go. "You're just a disciple," he told me many times after I complained to him about my progress. "How long have you been studying?"

"Four months," I'd answer. "Eight months, a year, two years." He'd shrug his shoulders and laugh.

"It takes time," he'd say. "I've been working on myself thirty years."

Most of my preconceptions vanished. I stopped looking at my world through a cracked glass. "Life has a way of smacking you across the head," he said to me many times, "a way of showing you real answers are exactly the opposite of what you think."

Q: Rudi died in an airplane crash. Could you speak a little more about that?

We took off from Teterboro Airport in New Jersey and flew north up the Hudson Valley to a small town near Albany. The plane got caught in dense fog, a fog so thick we couldn't see twenty feet in front of us. About a half-hour into the flight, we hit a mountain. There were four of us in the Cessna crash that killed Rudi instantly: Beau Buchanan (the pilot), Mimi Shore, Rudi, and myself. The rest of us survived. We spent a February night on top of the mountain, and then walked down at the crack of dawn. At the moment of the crash, I felt Rudi's soul pass into my body. I believe, to this day, that's the only reason I'm alive. He passed his soul force into me. He gave me his life and his teachings at that moment.

Q: What were his last words?

"A deeper sense of surrender." Those were his last words on Earth.

Q: That's a big part of what you teach?

Of course. Surrender teaches you to go deeper into yourself; it teaches you to let go. Rewards are steps on a ladder that connects the Earth with higher energy in the universe. They are not ends in themselves. They become traps if treated as ends; they become limitations to spiritual growth. There's no limitation to higher creative energy in the universe. The only limitation is the human mind, which holds on to rewards because they appear to represent security.

Q: You met a rare individual with the ability to help you. You studied with him until the moment of his death. I wonder if most of us can count on chance occurrences like this to happen?

A person who needs a spiritual life will find a teacher. It's a matter of evolution. When you're ready, the teacher will be there. Most people are not ready. It doesn't matter what they say. Their words sugarcoat deeper meanings; their words rarely, if ever, tap real spiritual need. It's like Liza Doolittle in My Fair Lady: "Words, words, words/I'm so sick of words ... show me." I don't listen anymore to people's rationalizations. I just tell them, "Your hunger isn't strong enough."

People are born to be happy, yet rarely, if ever, do you meet a happy person. Most people wallow in their own insecurity. They use it as a defense against growing up, an excuse to defeat themselves, to never trust teachers, gurus, anyone who can help them get closer to God. They leech on to mediocrity. It's safe; it's secure; it poses no threat to houses of cards built from ego, no threat to self-satisfied, well-patinated existences, to middle-class life insurance plans, to poverty-stricken, piss-poor, downtrodden victims of social malfunction, to any image we have of ourselves. Mediocrity reigns supreme. It's a god in its own right. People pray to it, genuflect before its altars, and consider it a gilded path through life.

A spiritual life is a different thing. It doesn't negate success, marriage, family, friendships, money, power, and fame. It puts them in their true perspective. They are steps on a ladder that extends into the cosmos, that connects every human being with God. They are not ends in themselves, but means to learn about oneself and one's karma.

There's another element as well. A human being's use of will to dictate external events is an attempt to create substance where there is none. The more he tries, the deeper he enmeshes himself in illusive quagmires. Pain deepens, neurosis spreads, unhappiness gets rampant, and the whole three-ringed circus gets bogged down in bullshit. The self is lost to neon glitter that reflects distorted well-being. It loses sight of what's really important.

Suffering forces people to reevaluate their lives, to search for new answers to timeless questions, to touch a part of themselves in need of spirituality. Hunger for that kind of food initiates an inner search. It's the first step in a lifelong voyage to the realms of the divine.

Q: Why do we need to meditate? Can you tell us about your approach to meditation?

There are no prerequisites for the meditation I teach. I ask people one thing: do they want to grow spiritually? If they want to have a spiritual life, then my meditation practice will work for them, but it doesn't come easy. It is not that I set barriers between a human being and their spiritual enlightenment. Those barriers are already there. Everyone suffers; everyone has thoughts and emotions; everyone hides behind defective parts of themselves. All I ask for is a committed effort to grow. Without that, a spiritual life is impossible. The rest is a learning process: How to use the mind properly, how to use the breath properly; where to focus; where to find balance, harmony, joy; how to be rooted; how to develop holistically; and how to keep working no matter the pain, pressure, and difficulty of living.

We have to survive ourselves. We are the problem. We're also the solution. When we get to the other side of ourselves, we connect consciously to God or higher energy in the universe.

Q: Why do you practice eye-open meditation?

The eyes make up the doorway to the human soul. They take in vast quantities of spiritual energy during meditation class— energy that works on the chakra system; which quiets the mind; opens the throat, heart, and navel chakras. Then the energy is consciously drawn through the sex chakra to the base of the spine where it activates kundalini. The force of kundalini rises to the crown of the head, opens the crown chakra, and lets the human soul force connect with higher energy in the universe. The person that teaches meditation class transmits *shakti* to the group, a strong catalyst that helps students go deeper within themselves.

There are three things going on in meditation class. First, the will is internalized. We use the mind and breath to open the chakra system. Second, open eyes keep us in touch with the world. We don't drift off to Never Land. Third, higher energy, or God, or whatever you want to call it, creates wholeness from the inner and outer dimensions of reality. We realize there's no separation, no barrier between inner, outer, and higher energies. It's like an equidistant triangle. It's all one contiguous flow of spirit. I often walk the New York streets and listen to the cry of spiritually famished people, to multitudes of undernourished souls that grope through life like inmates in a concentration camp, like refugees in Sudan or Ethiopia. It's not physical food they crave. Most of them are overweight porkers quite content with themselves. It's spiritual food they hunger for, something to quiet the mind and the emotions, to bring balance and harmony to life. They don't know where to get it.

If you want to learn to play a musical instrument, I'd think as I continued to walk, it's necessary to find a teacher. If you want to be a merchant, a lawyer, a doctor, plumber, anything, you have to learn it from somebody who's mastered the craft. When it comes to learning about ourselves, we're bankrupt. We think we know it all; we think there's nothing else to learn. We listen to a confused mind dictate right and wrong. Then we follow our own mad conclusions. Congested with inadequate knowledge, with fear, insecurity, guilt, and hundreds of other cast members of our prime-time soap opera, we refuse to listen to people who've mastered life's craft. We refuse to surrender a lifetime of preconception, of dogma, of conditioning, of rightness. We refuse to break down inner walls. As long as we cling to these walls, no one can ever teach us about God and enlightenment.

Q: Can you tell us a bit about your book, Leah?

Leah is a fictional tale (based in part on some truth) of a young girl who had terminal cancer, a tale told from the point of view of David, a healer and meditation teacher, and friend to Leah and Leah's mother. It's the story of a thirteen-year-old girl who's been told by doctors she's going to die in three weeks. She has an inoperable and untreatable tumor in her gut. It's a story of healing and meditation and miracle gone awry, a David-and-Goliath type story in which the impossible becomes possible. It's a voyage through the inner workings of a human being, through the chakra system and meridians, a spiritual voyage that reveals how proper use of energy can overcome terminal illness. David's train of thought, his stream of consciousness, pinpoints the source of disease. He shows the reader how to transform cancer into positive energy.

The problem is not cancer. The problem is people who have cancer and people who surround them. Disease is a way of people saying, "I hurt; help me. I want to be loved." Leah grew tired of being a porcelain vase or a petit-point textile adorned with superficial caresses—an object of human indifference. So "she put a little cancer in their lives." Her disease got the attention of her mother and her mother's lover. Her bankrupted emotional and spiritual state cried out for love so essential to living.

Children reach out to their parents for love. More often than not, the parents reject them. The parents are too busy, too frazzled, too neurotic, too full of themselves, too frightened or unhappy and beset by financial and emotional turmoil, to hug and kiss children, to be there for them in time of difficulty. Illness is a real attention-getter and terminal illness is the greatest attention-getter of all. It's a way to get sympathy, care, superficial love, and undivided attention. It's a way to get chicken soup dispensed with the love and guilt buried in the human heart. Hospitals are full of love-starved people. If we loved ourselves, if we found self-worth and joy inside, if we were able to live happy lives, ninety percent of the world's illnesses would disappear.

Q: How long after her healing did Leah live?

About a year and a half. She could have lived much longer. She and her mother had to change old patterns; to leave behind situations that helped create the disease in the first place; to learn to love unconditionally; to have a spiritual life; to work inside themselves to develop strong chakra systems, balance, harmony, and the strength to transform negative energy into a life-giving force. Tension does not go away. Problems do not go away. We have to master our inner lives, quiet the mind and emotions, and learn to use our garbage like a gardener learns to use compost. As I said before, the problem is not cancer, or any disease for that matter; it's the people who have the disease and the people who surround them. If they're willing to change, if they're willing to transform illness into a spiritual life, they can overcome most any ailment.

If people want to live, they won't accept banal answers to

life-threatening problems; they'll break through the veil of confusion, illusion, ignorance, and ineptitude that surrounds them. It's not just saying: "I want to live, I want to live, I want to live," then continuing to indulge in lifestyles that are killing you in the first place.

Q: But how do you teach people that?

A person has to be ready to learn. The Bible talks about "throwing pearls before swine." Most people are deaf to life's lessons. They listen only to the confusion in their addled brains. If cancer, heart conditions, AIDS, poverty, pain, and intense suffering do not penetrate thick walls of human defense, then nothing will. Human beings change only when they want to change. No words, sermons, or lectures on right ways of living are going to unclog diseased inner pipes. Love, compassion, patience, and forgiveness are tools that allow us to deal with ignorance, but the day ill people take disease and use it to have a spiritual life, that day, and only that day, will they be healed. It's better to live one full minute of life than eighty boring, unproductive, banal years rampant with mediocrity. If you die, so what? Everyone's got to die sometime. The problem is living and learning to be happy. Death is a serious problem because people haven't fully lived their lives.

Q: What do you say to people who don't take spiritual matters seriously?

Nothing. There's nothing to say to them. Life is a tough taskmaster. If they don't learn from life, they're certainly not going to learn from me.

Q: How does the concept of "New Age" fit into all this?

Many people use the idea of "New Age" to keep themselves from doing spiritual work. They get caught up in hoopla instead of deep meditation practice. There are thousands of paths to choose from, each employs holier-than-thou ad agencies to hard-sell spiritual fabric softener, but few, if any, give insight into the difficulty of meditation practice. They sell a product in the best Madison

Avenue tradition. People get sucked in. They're attracted to glitter, to ends not means, to Baba Dabarumdum's crystal aura in vegetarian paradise, to clothes, smells, food products, to far-out and groovy groups of similar-looking, similarly clad new agers that desperately try to conform to something, to pie-in-the-sky realities that help them escape the difficulty of dredging up their own garbage, to anything that avoids straight-on, no-bullshit work that clears an inner path to God.

Psychic and magical gifts are not necessarily spiritual gifts. They're often low-level cosmic energies used by people to control others. They're only tools. If we can surrender them, they help us get closer to God. The key to spiritual work is surrender of ego, self-image, rightness and wrongness—static that interfers with our link to infinite energy in the universe. The mind needs to get quiet, and the heart needs to open. We need to witness life's spectacle without zealots that judge the actions of others. It's like Christ said, "Who's going to throw the first stone?" Not me. Not anyone I know if they're honest with themselves. We've all a little Mary Magdalene in us. But the world's full of quick-tempered zealots that judge each other, self-righteous carpetbaggers that stuff the Lord down each other's throats, blind and half-crazed men and women who never learn "less is more," that selflessness is a sure path to enlightenment. They're trapped in their own image of God, in a fifteen-round slugfest in which "Mr. Right" and "Mr. Right" toe-to-toe it until neither have energy to get off the canvas. It's the dead battling the dead in a never-ending war of wills.

Q: *The dead battling the dead?*

Yes. People maneuvering in a paradoxical world replete with answers to most questions, people that struggle to justify their own positions, to prove a point of view no matter what price needs to be paid to convince someone else of their rightness. There are seven billion people on Earth. Each sees the world differently. No wonder everything's so crazy, no wonder conflicting ideas defy all reason. I rarely, if ever, meet a person humble enough to admit being wrong, a person who wishes to make up the difference, who wishes to learn from life, who admits he knows nothing. The wiser you get, the less you know, the greater the horizon, and the more opportunities there are to learn.

People covet commercial success. There's nothing wrong with this. It's just another form of energy. But if money is worshipped as an end in itself, it becomes one more idol in a pile of graven images. In today's world, the mind's power attaches itself to economic forces that sacrifice human life to mega-corporations like ancient biblical characters sacrificed cattle to God. Though ego will never disappear, though there's no Never Land of utopian communities without conflict on Earth, though people will always find reasons to fight with each other, there are options to life's strange duality. Either we master our inner lives, either we learn to use mind and emotion consciously, or we have to accept eternal servitude to human madness. Either we finally accept the world as it is, or we spend a lifetime bitching about things impossible to change. It doesn't take a genius to see what's wrong with life. It takes an extraordinary person to be happy, to be full of love, to be balanced and joyful. It takes an extraordinary person to see God in both positive and negative situations and be grateful to both. People have many limitations that make their lives more interesting. If we were all perfect, there'd be nothing to learn. We'd live in a static and boring world. Here's where love and compassion come into play. First, we've got to build inner lives, then find our self-worth, then love ourselves, and, finally, stop judging other people. We've got to learn to let the world be.

Q: Will daily meditation practice help to do this?

Frankly, it's the only way I know to do it. It doesn't necessarily have to be my meditation practice, which, I'm happy to say, is not for everyone. But some kind of discipline is necessary, something to get people to sit down and work on themselves every day, something to remind them to develop an inner life. Either we pay for our lives consciously or we pay for our lives unconsciously. It's one way or the other. The whole trick is to learn to use suffering consciously. It won't go away, so we might as well master it. We might as well use it to get closer to spiritual enlightenment.

CHAPTER TWO:

The Fundamental Elements of Spiritual Work

Spiritual work brings together life's discordant elements and creates harmony where there is none. The final goal is oneness with God. The journey from point A to point B is fraught with obstacles. I've heard many teachers say, "When I got my enlightenment..." I rarely hear teachers talk about thousands of enlightenments, one following the other, a chain that connects meditation practitioners with higher energy in the universe. Enlightened people do not know they are enlightened. They just live that way. If I'm enlightened, I've often thought with a smile on my face, then I've arrived at a place where growth stops. I'm enlightened! Then what! I bask in my aura of truth. I provide suntan lotion to less fortunate disciples. I berate them because they've yet to become enlightened. To get to God, an enlightened person has to surrender his enlightenment. If he doesn't, he'll return to the Earth for as many incarnations as it takes to learn that the best we can do every day is grow. God is infinite energy in the universe. To be one with God is to expand our consciousness so that when we leave the Earth nothing is left of us, not even consciousness. We are in a state of total surrender.

There are many dimensions to spiritual work, but its most fundamental aspect is three-dimensional. The first dimension is the internalization of energy; it's building a strong chakra system, thereby strengthening our connection with higher energy in the universe. This has nothing to do with intellectual or factual knowledge. To talk about chakras, to analyze them, to design color charts and to write insightful scientific and literary comparisons between chakras and parallel organs in the body or symbols in literature does not get us an iota closer to a strong inner life. It's mostly intellectual gibberish that waters down real experience.

Chakras are spiritual muscles. They need to be strengthened through proper use of mind and breath; they need to be developed by daily meditation practice. They need to be worked on until they remain permanently open. If not, they atrophy like any unused muscle; they waste until nothing is left.

The second dimension of spiritual work is staying in touch with the world. We live on Earth. Hundreds of situations test us every day, some positive, others negative, but all a manifestation of higher energy. If we stay balanced, we learn to realize there's no separation between our inner and outer lives. They reflect each other. They teach us about limitation, about the work necessary to free ourselves from obstacles, about the "I am" that struggles to get free, about karma and all its ramifications. We need the world. To reject it is to isolate ourselves in preconception.

For example, in my meditation practice, both student and teacher work with their eyes open. This simple technique keeps them in touch with life, because the eyes are a window into the soul. They absorb great quantities of energy into the chakra system, and when the mind is centered in the chakra right below the navel—the seat of balance, of foundation and real strength in a human being—the eyes and mind allow us to be in two places at the same time. When we apply this discipline to daily life, every situation is approached from centeredness. We maintain balance no matter what is going on. We see higher creative energy manifesting in every situation. We're capable of staying quiet and, at the same time, we can take care of the business of life.

The third element is higher energy. If the chakra system is open, then the spiritual force can expand the heart and throat and navel centers, quiet the mind, and transform tension into energy that activates kundalini and allows the soul force of a human being to unite with God. We discover there's no separation between inner and outer, higher and lower. It's all one energy, the energy of God—an equilateral triangle that connects three dimensions of consciousness. The outer world reflects our inner life. It changes as we change inside. We stop blaming life and take full responsibility for all our actions. It's the first step on a path that leads to spiritual enlightenment.

The Three Dimensions of Consciousness

One cannot exist without the other two. If we separate them, illusion and reality play funny games with our heads. We get blind, deaf, and dumb to spiritual matters. We think the inner and outer worlds are separate entities at odds with each other, enemies that plot sordid misadventures to entrap us in life-threatening situations. Confusion reigns. We become servants of the mind's mad sanatorium. The triangle I speak of is no different than Christian concept of Father, Son, and Holy Spirit. In fact, most religions use the triangle in some form or other, be it Hinduism, Sufism, Buddhism, Judaism, or Christianity. The triangle always plays an important part in the development of consciousness.

There are basic elements to meditation practice. For instance, by using the tools we're born with (mind and breath) to open the chakra system, then we actively build a strong inner life. The point of meditation is to experience higher consciousness. Reading about religion, chakras, occult sciences, and healing will introduce us to the possibilities of a spiritual life. Meditation is experiential. It is more than possibility. Practiced on a regular basis, it connects our consciousness to infinite energy in the universe. Improper practice can do more harm than good. It's why we need to study with men and women who've mastered the craft of inner work, who serve higher energy by teaching needy disciples to open inside.

The chakra system, though considered esoteric and occult, is no more esoteric or occult than the digestive system or the excretory system or the respiratory system. Its well-being is essential to human life. It needs care and attention. Each chakra is the seat of some form of higher consciousness. The mind, for instance, is the center of knowledge and wisdom; the heart, of love, gratitude and joyfulness; the navel area, of foundation and balance; the sex chakra, of transformation; the base of the spine, of kundalini—the soul or life-giving force that strives to get to God.

The Throat and Sexual Chakras

The throat chakra is our means of communication. If the throat chakra isn't open, most verbal exchange is like static on a radio. People talk at each other, not to each other. They don't talk from a state of openness; they talk from a state of congestion and despair and unhappiness. Communication is impossible. The throat chakra is the center of sound. The Bible says, "In the beginning was the Word." That Word gives birth to all creation, so every word we utter is a reflection of how close we are to God, of how open we are, of how spiritually evolved we've become. Mostly, we take words for granted. They emit tension, unhappiness, deep suffering, and create around us a world that reflects our neurotic state of being.

The sex chakra transforms humanity into spirit by giving birth to our spiritual selves. It's the essence of tantra or the yoga of transformation, the means whereby conceptual knowledge, tension, the seen and unseen world, and life itself, is transformed into an energy force that activates kundalini. As we draw energy from the navel area through the sex chakra to the base of the spine, we awaken the serpent soul within us, an energy force that burns life's tensions, then rises to the crown chakra where it gathers, ripens, then opens the crown and moves to higher planes of consciousness. The marriage of the human soul and the Universal Soul gives birth to a river of conscious energy that returns to the chakra system. First it enters the brain (third eye), then the throat, heart, etc. This recycled energy is the beginning of a spiritual life. It brings knowledge, wisdom, love, joy, foundation, tantric mastery, Om (the sound of creative energy in the universe), and all elements of higher consciousness.

Without joy and love and gratitude, we're more animalistic than human. Without strong inner foundation, we are incapable of supporting spiritual energy, the most powerful energy that exists in the universe.

In the Bhagavad-Gita, Krishna reveals himself to Arjuna. He talks about the light of a thousand suns that appear in the sky, of the entire human race rushing headlong into fire, of energy more powerful, more unimaginable, and more omnipotent than anything the human mind can comprehend. The vision Krishna describes (as powerful as it may be) is perhaps the small toe of God. He's not talking about wimpy, holier-than-thou, lackluster energy. He's talking about creation from the beginning to the end of time, about what exists before and after Genesis and Armageddon, about aeons of light and fire that transcends all human comprehension. The chakra system is the link to all this. It's connected to very powerful energies, but first we have to learn to be human. Then, we further develop a chakra system strong enough to channel God's energy. It's easy to forget that we're born on Earth and that we have responsibilities. We have karma to work out, service to do, and we've got to learn to love and be happy and to separate what's real from what's an illusion.

The Pandora's Box of Daily Living

The Earth's a complex university with multifarious departments all eager to teach us how to get to God. The problem is we don't listen. We know better than the Earth. We argue with a great master, an argument impossible to win, but an argument that engages most of our time and energy—and finally exhausts us. The energy needed to develop a spiritual life is wasted on pettiness, vanity, greed, avarice, and empty desire; on personal theatrics magnified by mindsets conditioned to worship superficial things, none of which makes us happy, all of which fills a ludicrous void in the pit of humanity's stomach.

When a human being's happy, he or she has learned everything to be learned on Earth. I know this sounds simplistic, but try it. Try to live with an open heart. I've met brilliant people, rich people, psychically gifted people, but, rarely, if ever, have I met a happy person. It's like finding a fifty-carat clear diamond in a muddy pond.

We chose to be born On Earth. We came to learn the lessons to be learned: how to work out karma, how to finally free ourselves from pain and suffering. Why deny this? Why hide in neurotic frenzy? Why not be happy? Why not separate illusion from reality and be one with creative energy in the universe? It's stupid, don't you think, to postpone the inevitable, to substitute junk food for a gourmet meal, to turn our backs on a spiritual life.

Meditation practice unifies the inner and outer dimensions of consciousness and makes us aware there's no separation between the two. They are part and parcel of the same force. The material world, economics, thought, emotion, good and evil, right and wrong, animal and vegetable life, Earth, stones, rocks, water, everything and anything we perceive is a manifestation of God's energy. Then the mind categorizes life. It separates things into compartments. It destroys unity, harmony, and balance and dwells on conflict, opposites, and battles that have little or no meaning in the course of history and time. We listen to the mind as if it were God. We follow its instructions over frenzied paths that lead to dead ends. We prefer tension to quiet, unhappiness to happiness, and sickness to well being. Why else do we wallow in them? We choose darkness over light and death over life, and our words, though well chosen and gilded with moral epithets, are nothing more than badly glued veneers on unstable and weather-worn dogma. Though we bandy about words like organic, natural, and holistic, we rarely associate them with an inner life or strong chakra system or the use of mind and breath to effectively connect our consciousness to God.

Meditation is a craft, and its tools are mind and breath, tools that most people haven't learned to use properly. Breath is like prayer. Every time we inhale, we receive life, and every time we exhale, we surrender a part of ourselves. The mind's power opens the foundation of our being. It brings harmony and balance, and it helps us develop strong inner lives. It transforms tension into a life-giving force. The question remains, how to do this? The answer is simple. It takes training. We have to submit ourselves to the rigors of yoga. We have to discipline ourselves in the ways of meditation. We have to master organic elements like mind and breath.

God exists both in the world and outside the world. If we're not conscious of God in the humdrum of day-to-day activity, we're not going to find Him in more esoteric realms. An enlight-ened person does both. He's like a saint in an El Greco painting: large feet planted firmly on Earth, elongated body that reaches from Earth to cosmic sky, and the fingers of an outstretched hand touching heaven.

The material world is an all-encompassing, pressure-filled Pandora's box of daily living with subtle planes of mind, psyche, emotions, economics, power, personality, image, and ego. All this constitutes the fabric of life. There's no escaping it. All these are constant reminders that we're born on Earth and not in seraphic realms or heavenly landscapes. We have karma to work out with parents, spouses, children, friends, relatives, and numerous other people we meet daily. But each day is a spectacle of creation, a precious God-given gift to be treasured from the moment we wake up in the morning to the moment we sleep. It's our day. If we scorn it, if we denigrate it, if we spend the day complaining, the spectacle of life passes us by, the moment is lost in anger, and the dull, angst-ridden debacle we flounder in blinds us to love and to higher energy in the universe. We live in a piss-pot of our own creation. We're blind, half-mad, and irrational creatures that drown in unhappiness. We're unable to find a way to make heads or tails of life's conundrum.

The material world's rewards attract us like neon lights above a gambling casino. We risk everything for a slice of the action, then learn, to our dismay, the action gives less than a shit if we live or die. At the appropriate time, human beings are discarded like banana peels. They're tossed onto a rubbish heap to be collected by a grim reaper who carts them away to retirement or Never Land or living death—old and useless, burned-out humanity too scared to do anything but sit and wait.

Though people detest age's debilitating presence, they also welcome rest and retirement and getting away from a frenzied life. But age is also an excuse to allow the mind and body to atrophy. Meditation practitioners become conscious that the inner life of a human being never grows old. The more developed the chakra system, the more opportunity there is to reverse the physical and mental aging process. There's a greater wellspring of energy to draw from. There's less confusion, more calm, more wisdom, discipline, and training. We're like ripe fruit ready to be plucked by God. The child in us matures into a newborn babe full of spiritual energy. The child in us isn't afraid to age or die. It's a strong child, free of anxiety and neurosis, conscious enough to separate illusion from reality. As our creative capacity grows with age, so does our wisdom and understanding of life and death. We're no longer trapped in material, emotional, mental, and sexual quandaries.

Meditation Practice

The karmic mirror reflects who and what we are. It doesn't lie. If we're not afraid to take a good look, it will teach us exactly what we have to do to change. We can revive the child in us, strengthen him, and let him develop into a mature and conscious human being. We'll stop blaming the world for our own limitations. We'll realize the older we get, the younger we get. The child in us never dies. Beyond material, mental, and emotional realities lies a transcendental plane, a *bardo*, the astral realm that consists of devas, angels, demigods, light, form, color, magic, dream, psychic manifestation—the whole cosmic can-can we connect to when the crown chakra opens and the soul of a human being moves into higher planes. The material plane is the densest energy. Structured and conceptual, its impenetrable wall conditions our minds into believing what we see is what the world is. Its density forms our consciousness. But the mind can break down material planes into component parts. It analyzes, reasons, grasps abstraction, and devises mathematical and scientific formulas and theorems that reduce matter to energy. The world's density dissolves into atomic particles that move about us.

Meditation works on the same principle. The mind is used to break down inner density, to transform psychological, emotional, and physical walls and obstacles into energy that ignites kundalini and fuels its rise into the astral, a place where gods, demigods, angels, seraphim, and all manner of strange and dreamlike creatures make their home. The goal is not to hang out with these creatures, but to learn from them, to absorb their energy and use it as fuel to transcend time and space. We want to enter realms of consciousness that defy anything the human mind can understand.

The astral is a cosmic slum, a low-level energy located just above the crown chakra. It is something like Las Vegas of the spiritual realm, full of glitter and glitterati, madcap demons and angels, a cool place to hang out, but a limitation to inner growth. It's the home of both black and white magic, psychic power, sorcery, whatever's necessary to control the lives of unwitting disciples. If astral energy is used to evolve spiritually, its force quickens the growth process. If its dark power is used to gain control over people, the practitioner becomes a danger to himself and the rest of the human race.

Meditation practice allows us to experience many dimensions of consciousness at the same time. Lower realms, like thought, emotion and matter are transformed into kundalini, which rises up the spine to the crown chakra and into the astral plane. Our emotional and mental garbage is transformed into gold. The tension that kills us becomes a life-giving energy. It helps us gain enlightenment. The process takes years of inner work. There are no quick paths, no shortcuts. We've got to hack our way through the psychic underbrush until we arrive at clearings, until we're no longer stuck on any ego level or plane of wisdom or understanding. Spiritual work requires total surrender.

Not everyone is equipped to do deep spiritual work. To try and force it down the throats of masses of people is a mistake. Those who've evolved to a place in themselves ready to listen to a spiritual master are few and far between. The work itself sifts through the field and determines who's going to get enlightenment and who will veer off into one of thousands of life's small compartments. It's all a process of evolution, of death and rebirth, of incarnation linked to incarnation until one's consciousness is ready to surrender everything. Until then, the *samsara* merry-go-round continues to spin, the music plays, and we marvel at every booth in the carnival.

The key to working in the astral or on cosmic levels is a strong foundation. The mind has to be focused in the *hara*. The *chi* needs to be balanced. If the mind drifts into astral planes, slums around there, and attaches itself to magical creatures or psychic energy, meditation practitioners can drive themselves crazy. There needs to be a root system, a point of reference, inner strength, and foundation. Astral energy is very strong. It can snap something in the brain. It can drive a person mad. The point isn't to hang out there! The point is to use the energy of the astral plane as a catalyst to build one's inner life. We can't be attached to dreams and visions. They're tools, and, like any other tool, they have a purpose, that purpose being the development of higher consciousness. They exist to help us become more human.

It's too easy to get caught up in the "far-out" elements of spiritual work. It's easy to forget we have karma and responsibility and day-to-day lives. It's easy to become a cosmic freak, an astral vaudevillian that puts on a magic show. Power is very attractive, and astral power is the most attractive of all. It can be used to enslave many people. It can be used to create false gods and false prophets. It can be used to inflate megalomaniacal teachers into pompous baboons doing quasi-spiritual work, but chakra systems have checks and balances. Humility, love, gratitude, each of these, is a safeguard against power. Each transforms cosmic madness into divine light.

The chakra system, like the Sephirotic Tree in Kabbalah, has branches that touch astral planes of consciousness. It also attracts light, energy, knowledge, wisdom, beauty, and visions of gods and demigods that live in the cosmos. But it's rooted in the *hara*, which is the third, or power, chakra located just below the navel. There we activate *chi*, an energy force that emanates from the third chakra and strengthens our foundation and allows us to maintain balance. The simple act of centering ourselves in the navel chakra keeps the power of kundalini from making us crazy. As we draw energy from the forehead to the throat, to the heart, to the navel area, to the sex chakra, and the base of the spine, the focus of the mind in the *hara* keeps us centered. It allows us to draw energy through the sex chakra and activate kundalini. Kundalini rises to the crown chakra. Then it moves into the cosmos and guides the meditation practitioner to a point in time and space where all creation comes into being, at once merging the human soul with higher energy where there's less ego and more God, more spirit and less conceptualization, and ultimately, *samadhi*, or enlightenment, the final goal of evolution.

The work of meditation creates wholeness in a human being. It strengthens our foundation, opens the heart and the throat, quiets the mind, unifies transcendental consciousness with life on Earth, and gives us the strength to be grateful, to endure, to have patience, forgiveness, and compassion no matter what goes on. It puts every situation in true perspective. It teaches us that life and death are links on a chain connected to Spirit; it teaches us that higher energy is in the world and outside the world at the same time. All we have to do is embrace it.

People say this is dangerous. It could be. But most anything's dangerous when undertaken without consciousness. If we develop the craft of meditation, if we learn from a master and we stay centered, then there's nothing dangerous about kundalini. What's dangerous is lack of centeredness, paucity of spiritual energy, and an undeveloped chakra system. Without spiritual training, we become slaves of our own psychic melodrama. Meditation helps us absorb, burn up, and transform tension into spirituality. This doesn't sound dangerous to me. It sounds wonderful!

The chakra system connects our consciousness to the source of creative energy in the universe. Meditation practice is no different than the craft of plumbing. The practitioner creates pipes that keep spiritual water flowing. If our pipes rust and corrode, the system stops working. It clogs up and congests and cuts us off from the well. We dry up, starve, suffer, and die unconsciously. We grovel at the feet of tension, always "strangers in a strange land." We waste away and blame the world for our pain, unhappiness, and spiritual malnourishment. We live and die in a wasteland of our own making.

The world is a dark and mysterious place, tense, enigmatic, and full of danger, and we hide from it, first within ourselves, then in tiny closets built from fear, well-insulated closets, safe closets, closets that protect us. We look out at a world full of tension. It reflects our own anxiety-ridden selves. But we are the world we see about us. There's no escaping it and nowhere to hide. The pain forces us to take action. We run to therapists, doctors, hypnotists, acupuncturists, and gurus. We run and run until there's nowhere else to run, until we realize that no one's going to do it for us. We have to learn to do it for ourselves. The craziness won't go away. It has taken root like weeds in a garden. Then a voice says, "There must be a way to clean up the mess." That's a beginning. The next step is to learn techniques of inner work, to sit down every day and apply them, to build the chakra system, to clean the rusty pipes, to get strong enough to see the world with some clarity.

The outer world reflects our inner lives, but it's a friend and a teacher. Wise men listen to teachers. They let teachers show them how to change; they let mirrored reflections guide them through labyrinthine networks of confusion. They try not to fight with their teacher. Since the act of listening requires surrender, it means we have to let go of preconceptions, of right and wrong ideas, of anything bolstering our ego. Then we make room inside ourselves for spiritual energy. Why fight with your teacher? Learn from him, grow because of his wisdom, re-examine your own limitations, and use them to build an inner life. It's easy to find excuses to stop working on oneself. Life's a caldron of malfeasance, a divine farce, a slapstick comedy that stars ditsy egomaniacs that trip all over each other. It's not hard to pick out bullshit. It's hard to keep one's mouth shut and continue to grow. It's hard to learn from the bullshit, to use it as compost in a private inner organic garden. We have to strengthen our spiritual lives by letting the outer world remind us what to do. We have to sustain spiritual growth no matter what problems face us.

The real problem is getting past oneself. This is something few people are willing to face. On the other side of anger, confusion, fear, anxiety, guilt, on the other side of the panoply of human thought and emotion, there's a spiritual life and freedom, a clear path to enlightenment.

Spirit creates wholeness from disparate threads of life. It takes mind, emotion, and matter and unifies them in a mandala of creation. There is no longer separation. We stop compartmentalizing oneness and see life evolve before our eyes. The chakra system's strength can transform everything into spirit. We no longer isolate ourselves in ego. We're no longer existential werewolves scenting prey. The Earth doesn't threaten our well-being. The ability to digest life's trauma gives us strength to see past illusion, to see that whatever exists within time and space is a trap, a transient, will-o'-the-wisp, a *Midsummer Night's Dream* performed by angels and sprites and semi-comatose pitch men, a wheel of life that needs to be greased, a gnomon that refuses to follow the sun. Responsibility falls on each and every human being. There is mind, breath, chakras, spirit, soul, and infinite energy in the universe. There is also skepticism, lack of trust, lack of forgiveness, ignorance, stupidity, and no desire to develop an inner life.

Human beings think they know everything, but they're in a constant struggle with death, and death inevitably wins. Death's a wisecracking, agile, moonfaced vaudevillian whose shriek fills every crevice on Earth. It dances all around us and never gives us a moment's rest. It plucks unripened souls from the Earth like a starving bird plucks newly-formed berries from a bush.

Human beings are unwittingly the victims of this struggle. As Christ said, "They know not what they do." They serve mutable laws that change moment to moment, that disrupt balance and harmony, and that are always in conflict. They reject God, or they accept Him in rational, well-worked-out theories that explain the unexplainable, in safe theories institutionalized by religious parrots that repeat stale aphorisms to congregations of well-meaning but frightened seekers after truth, aphorisms that take the soul out of religion.

It takes guts to have a spiritual life. You spend your time making the impossible possible. You learn to detach yourself from illusion. You learn to surrender totally to God, but not a rational God, not a God locked in the human mind, not a dogmatic, conceptualized God, but Infinite Energy in the Universe. He is a God that speaks in paradoxes, who exists in the world and outside the world at the same time, who defies earthly logic, a God who is above and beyond all human understanding, who frees us of our karma and ourselves.

There are no answers in books. They give clues, insights, and explanations, and they touch on truths, but no book, no matter how profound, can be substituted for experience. The harsh truth is that a spiritual life is an experiential thing. It's not to be found in the mind, or in tidbits of knowledge, nor insights, nor in reason and understanding. These are sylphs that float in space. They rarely, if ever, come down to Earth; they rarely, if ever, become part of practical experience. It takes balls to have a spiritual life, to one-pointedly work every day to get closer to God, to arrive at a place where you take nothing for granted.

Few people know what they're working for on Earth. Business, family, success, power, the whole laundry list of human need –– all of it forces people to lose sight of basic spiritual practice. "I have no time...I'm too busy...I've a date...a concert...a weekend in the country...I'm too busy spending my God-given energy to sit down and refuel my tank." Then age sets in, age and disease and an atrophied chakra system, and people wonder what happened, why youth vanished, why they no longer have the strength to live creative lives? The price is very dear.

A spiritual life denies us nothing, not family, friendships, business, leisure, success, nor any other of life's abundant treasures.

It just gives it all perspective. No single goal becomes an end in itself. Each is a step on a ladder, just another opportunity to learn to surrender to higher energy. Work becomes clear as both success and failure find their place in the design of the universe. People are very thick. It takes a long time for them to learn what's real. Pain, suffering, disappointment, and failure are important teachers on life's path, perhaps the most important. Without them, we'd do nothing about ourselves. We'd develop cabbage consciousness, flatulence, laziness, and self-satisfaction. The only thing that would expand is our rear ends. I've heard many wise men say, "Suffering is the quickest path to God." I believe that's true. Pain doesn't go away. It's God's gift to the wise, a reminder that we must work on ourselves every day.

The Male and Female Principles

The whole mystery of tantra is in masculine/feminine union, in sex and the power of sex internalized, and used to draw energy from the chakra below the navel to the base of the spine. This energy activates kundalini and makes possible a spiritual life.

Sexual intercourse could be the most profound meditation practice on Earth. If the chemistry is right, if both partners are serious practitioners of deep inner work, if both chakra systems are strong, and if the heart is open and there's love and joy, balance and harmony, each partner can aid the other in drawing sexual energy to the base of the spine. This simple act transforms human levels to spiritual levels. We give birth to ourselves; we surrender our humanity. We offer love, joy, gratitude, the whole karmic circus, the power of male/female union; we surrender everything unconditionally to God. Each partner aids the other at the moment of orgasm to ignite kundalini and draw its energy to the top of the head.

Tantric yoga can't be taught to undeveloped students. A person has to be ready. Time, evolution, and serious meditation practice prepare one for this extraordinary form of inner work. It is meditation on its highest levels, a merging of Shiva/Shakti, yin/yang, masculine/feminine principles, a union of opposites that creates harmony and balance within.

Most sex is an orgasmic dumping ground for tension, a

battleground for power, a subtle draining of energy, and a not-too-subtle way of people controlling each other, but tantra, practiced by highly-evolved meditation students, allows them to give and receive unconditionally. No one is drained. Both parties feel the power of higher energy working inside them. It's a pathway to freedom, a way to get to the other side of oneself.

One can practice tantra without a partner. During meditation, one must consciously draw energy through the sex chakra to the base of the spine. If this is done over and over again, the human will transform itself into the divine kundalini and rise to the top of our head.

It enables us to reach transcendental consciousness. For lack of better terminology, there's an inner erection that connects the navel chakra with the base of the spine where the female principle, or *shakti*, makes its home. This channel exists in both men and women. When energy moves from the navel area to the base of the spine, it gives birth to kundalini. When energy moves from the base of the spine to the navel area, it purifies the meditation practitioner's inner being. He gives birth to himself. It's kind of an immaculate conception.

Each chakra has a male/female counterpart that needs to be mated. When the heart chakra opens, for instance, and unifies its masculine and feminine parts, joy, gratitude, love, and all the higher emotions can be offered directly to God. There's a channel that connects the heart chakra to the top of the head. That's the pathway gratitude takes directly to the realm of higher energy in the universe. The same process takes place in the forehead, throat, navel area and sex area. In each chakra, union of opposites heals the practitioner.

Spiritual energy moves downward through each chakra to the base of the spine, then up the spine to the crown. It completes a full cycle that nurtures and develops all facets of our humanity, one that transforms the human into kundalini that merges with God. There are direct links between the third eye and the crown chakra, the navel and the base of the spine, the throat and the crown, the sex and the force of kundalini. Most of this sounds like theory, but when meditation practitioners experience the miracle of an inner life, mental and emotional muck disappears and spiritual energy opens channels to higher planes of consciousness.

Tantra, that strangely mysterious yogic teaching, becomes integral to everyday living. The male/female principle is no longer an interesting idea read about in spiritual guidebooks. It becomes a technique that advanced inner work practitioners can use to hasten spiritual development. The Shiva/Shakti marriage is the most important marriage of male/female energy on Earth. Without it, a spiritual life is impossible; without it, our energy grows stagnant and the lotus flower never emerges from the mud.

The spiritual process is a complicated network of inner realizations made simple through meditation. Its hieroglyphics are decoded by an experiential step-by-step refinement of inner confusion. There'll always be conflict in people because no one's perfect. That in itself keeps the human race striving for higher consciousness.

The lack of perfection is a God-given blessing discounted by most people. They don't like discomfort, mistakes, physical pain, and mental and emotional insecurity. They don't like it that the human race is slightly off-balance. Who can blame them? Only a madman takes pleasure in pain. Without patience, compassion, the fortitude to survive, and the ability to forgive ourselves and others, and, most importantly, without self-worth, it's difficult for a human being to live a peaceful life. Discomfort and pain shouldn't dishearten us. They should inspire us to work harder on ourselves.

Adversity is a great tool in the hands of people who desire enlightenment, people who realize perfection on Earth is an impossibility. Only God is perfect. The best a human being can do is grow closer to God every day of his life. Harmony and balance are simply goals to be attained. If they don't exist at the moment, so what! So we haven't arrived. We can still take joy in the work to be done.

Human beings excel at demanding perfection from others. When it comes to their own inner lives, few, if any, can claim some degree of clarity. It's rare to find a person with a quiet mind. But people who complain, who find fault with others and who run off at the mouth, are a dime a dozen. Perfection's a very high state of being, something to strive for in oneself, a state of total surrender, oneness with God, and the end product of a lifetime of spiritual work.

The Womb of the Mother

Each practitioner of meditation experiences spiritual growth differently. Though people practice the same meditation craft, rarely, if ever, do their inner experiences resemble the experience of others on the same spiritual path. Thank God we're all different. It would be horrible to see clones of myself sitting in meditation classes.

A human being can fight his way out of hell. History has shown that murderers can become saints, that thieves can become holy men, and that magicians can become men of God. Change is the cornerstone of spiritual work's ongoing process that links moment to moment. Its force defies human logic. It demands consciousness of how energy manifests on Earth, how life evolves, how no two days truly resemble each other. But there's no defining change.

Every generation grapples with the lower depths. Mankind has survived concentration camps, prisons, ghettos, famine, plague, racial and religious persecution, fascist and totalitarian states, death squads, and torture chambers. Horrific cries of pain pierce the pearly gates and make God sit up and take notice of "man's inhumanity to man." But for some incomprehensible reason cruelty doesn't go away. Men kill each other, torture each other and subject each other to pain. The history of mankind can be summed up in Edvard Munch's painting called *The Shriek*. Intolerable suffering goes unheeded by viewers of the painting who are trapped in their own futile and absurdly painful lives — a shriek that comes directly from the heart of every human being, but fills a museum's gallery with edgy silence.

It doesn't matter where a man comes from if he works on himself every day to grow and change. There's nothing worse than stagnant energy. It's about as close to hell as life gets on Earth.

In times of trauma, mankind almost always turns to God. Churches and synagogues fill up to capacity, and *Kyrie Eleisons* rise fervently into cloudy skies. People want answers, but there are none. There's just a day-by-day struggle to free oneself of karma's clutches. There's just the grind of spiritual work that gets us closer to the source of creation, to the womb of the Mother Goddess who gives birth to life, to the genesis of time and space, and to the inception of all things.

In Calcutta, at the temple of Dakshineswar, while sitting in deep meditation, I heard the spirit voices of Ramakrishna and Sarada Devi. They told me to listen to the Mother Goddess. I had no idea what they meant, but, subsequently, after many months of meditation practice, I realized the Mother Goddess is the spectacle of creation around me. I can't listen to Her voice if I'm not fully alive in the moment, if my mind's dwelling on the past or future. I realized that Genesis isn't some point in history millions of millennia ago. Genesis is this moment. It's the universe creating and recreating itself in the present. The voice of the Mother Goddess frees us from ourselves. It teaches us to tame the mind and to be one with life's ever-changing spectacle. She is Creation made manifest, and we are her children. We're in her womb waiting to be born. The marriage of our soul with the Mother Goddess touches a point in time and space where all creation comes into existence.

The question always is: how does one transform metaphysical insights into a practical approach to life? We live on earth, not in the cosmos, and esoteric principles mean nothing if they can't be used in a pragmatic way. It's one thing to say that we must surrender everything to higher energy in the universe; it's one thing to say that we need different priorities and that we are supposed to live in the world and be free of the world at the same time; and I'm sad to say, this is nothing more than a vast accumulation of words if people are incapable of transforming these words into reality. We shouldn't dwell on words like karma and try to figure out how to free ourselves from it's invisible prison; we shouldn't dwell on or try to figure out what it means to be of service in life, or what it means to be responsible to ourselves and other people. If there's success in life, there will also be failure; if there's good there will also be evil. Trying to figure out how energy manifests on earth tires the brain and often leads us nowhere. It's simply a matter of learning to "be." But the question is: how do we do this? It's a difficult question, but one that's key to inner peace, to joy and love, and to our evolution as human beings.

We must start with basic meditation techniques that quiet the mind, that open the heart, that center us in the third chakra. If we use them to transform our neurotic selves to a state of inner quiet; if use them to stop pandering a "little boy blue" image of self that peeks out at the world from self imposed delusion; if we stop using neurosis as an excuse to not function, if there's inner balance and harmony and we can like ourselves, we've taken a major step in learning how to become human. The esoteric becomes practical. As long as we're crazy, we don't have to take responsibility for anything. We never grow up. A seven-year-old child inhabits the body of an adult. He's an emotional dwarf, an intellectual Lilliputian; tense and unhappy, he makes life impossible for people close to him.

They say God is love, but it's impossible to connect with God's love if we live without self worth, and are not happy. If we quell our inner dragons and open our heart, we free ourselves from the one person who keeps us from being happy, the only person we spend twenty-four hours a day with, and, strange as it may sound, remains life's greatest mystery. All too often, we look into the mirror, and see that person, but rarely, if ever, do we look past surface levels of tension that hide deeper perceptions of self. If we free our self from inner conflict and live fully in the moment, it's possible to witness the Mother Goddess's spectacle of creation. She is the ever-present miracle of life creating and recreating itself within us and in the world we see around us.

The soul of a human being evolves through hundreds, if not thousands of lifetimes before it's ready to merge with God. Time is a non-factor. Each incarnation is a study course in a different department in life's university. There are young souls, old souls, middle-aged souls, all kinds of souls that walk around on Earth. No soul is in competition with any other soul. All of them evolve, learn, and are part of a greater design. Some souls crawl like snails. Others gallop like stallions, but each learns exactly what it's on Earth to learn.

The ultimate goal of evolution is spiritual enlightenment, and God (Higher Creative Energy) has enough patience to wait for every soul to come home. When people are ready, higher energy finds them. It sends them everything they need to grow spiritually. When they're not ready, it waits. Why scold children? They're in enough pain as it is. They can only hear what they're ready to hear. The question is, how do we know we're ready? We don't.

The process is an organic evolution of consciousness. One day we find ourselves listening to an inner voice; we find ourselves meditating. We discover spiritual food is essential for our well-being. The whole cosmic comedy begins to make sense. There's nothing illogical about the need to return to the womb of creation.

The transcendence of material, emotional, and mental problems are the beginning of a long journey to God. Once we get free of neurosis and assume full responsibility for ourselves, once we master our inner lives and can transform tension into *chi*, we are open enough for the universe to use us as vehicles that transmit *Shakti*. Our real work on Earth begins. Neurosis is no longer an excuse. We have to be responsible to higher energy, to ourselves, and to people in our lives. We have to surrender whatever the mind understands.

The marriage of the human soul with the Divine Mother Goddess gives birth to a child who's welcomed into realms of consciousness that transcend time and space. It's the final goal of spiritual work, a oneness with God, the only real freedom. The Mother Goddess gives birth to everything in the universe. She also takes it away. We die, don't we, and death, the blind spot in every human being, the equalizer that reduces empires to six-foot plots of land, is the servant of the Mother Goddess. It forces us to surrender everything. It puts life in its true perspective, then drives us to work on ourselves, to deepen our inner lives, and to become more conscious of reality's subtle nature.

Psychic powers, black or white magic, and any form of astral megalomania that attaches itself to ego are tools to control people on Earth, dangerous tools used to enslave innocent spiritual seekers. Many gurus use these tools. They cannot surrender their position. They don't realize a true teacher must give his teachings away. If he doesn't, the teachings become another umbilical cord that attaches him to Earth.

A spiritual thread connects the human soul to the Universal Soul, a thread that connects each and every one of us to Creation. Life emerges from the womb of the Mother Goddess, and consciousness (the thread) allows us to return to the Mother who gave birth to us in the first place. Consciousness allows us to marry the Mother and enter realms outside of time and space. Each and every soul on Earth evolves towards the Mother, each in its own time until life and death disappear and there's only nothingness. It's the marriage of Shiva and Shakti, Jehovah and *Shekinah*, God and the Virgin Mary, the mystical marriage that gives birth to spiritual enlightenment.

That's why we meditate. It's a step-by-step refinement of consciousness that guides us. We work on ourselves to get free of mind and emotion, the body, the psyche, the astral, time and space, the Mother, and all Her Creation. We work on ourselves until nothing's left but oneness with God. Everything else is consumed by the universe. We are free!

Life on Earth is mostly about power, money, and relationships––goals that should not be ends in themselves but steps on a ladder to enlightenment. If they become ends in themselves, they consume our vital force; they dry us up and make our bodies breeding grounds for disease and tension. A strong chakra system helps to detach us from lesser goals. It creates foundation, balance, joy, love, clarity of mind and emotion, simplicity, and the ability to distinguish between what's real and what's an illusion. The ego dissolves in a strong chakra system. We no longer judge what's right or wrong. We live in a state of surrender.

The Mechanics of the Chakra System and Kundalini

Chakras are psychic muscles that link a human being with higher creative energy in the universe, muscles that need to be worked every day to keep them from atrophying. When the chakra system is open, spiritual energy acts like Drano. It unclogs our inner pipes. It disinfects garbage that floats in stagnant parts of ourselves, regenerates our life force, and creates balance and harmony. If the chakra system is closed, our life force is like a drip from a leaky faucet. There's barely enough energy to get through the day. Through meditation, we learn to open and strengthen the chakra system. We absorb more energy, heal ourselves of psychological and physical illness, and learn to detach ourselves from illusion and to connect our consciousness with higher energy in the universe.

As I said earlier, chakras are located in different parts of the body. There's one in the center of the forehead, sometimes called the third eye. There's one in the throat, the heart, right below the navel, in the genitals, at the base of the spine, and at the top of the head. Each one of these chakras represents a different aspect of our humanity. For instance, the third eye, or chakra, at the center of the forehead is the seat of knowledge, wisdom, and choice. When that chakra opens, we can separate illusion from reality. The throat is the center of sound and communication, our ability to relate to other people. When it's open, our words have deeper meaning. If not, communication is like static on a radio. We speak in half-thoughts and vague ideas, and little, if anything, is communicated to the listener. It's why most conversation sounds like babble.

The heart is the seat of love, joy, gratitude, and the whole spectrum of higher and lower emotions. The chakra below the navel is the center of foundation, power, and stability, the *chi* located in the *hara* that gives balance to life. The chakra in the sexual area is the seat of transformation. The tantric force in the sex chakra transforms the human to the divine and activates the dormant kundalini in the chakra at the base of the spine — the creative force needed by the soul so it can rise to the chakra at the crown of the head, open that chakra, move into astral planes of consciousness, and merge with the Mother Goddess at the source of creation.

The tools of meditation are mind and breath—mind being our strongest instrument, and breath, the spirit moving in and out of our bodies. We're born with these tools, but few, if any of us know how to use them properly.

Chakras atrophy like any other muscle in the body. They have to be strengthened through proper use of mind and breath. If you don't use a refrigerator, it'll waste away. If you don't use a car, it goes to pot. If you don't use muscles, they turn to flab. If we don't use the chakra system, it too will waste away. Meditation practice is more than sitting quietly with your eyes closed; it's more than relaxation. It's the conscious use of mind and breath to open chakras, strengthen them, and build a direct connection between ourselves and higher energy in the universe. We need to strengthen the chakra system so it's permanently open, so it can continue to absorb the flow of infinite energy that pours out of the cosmos like Niagara Falls and not like a leaky faucet.

Each of the seven basic chakras is connected to the spine, and the spine is the only area in a human being where energy rises. If you open the heart chakra, spiritual energy moves through the heart to the spine. When it touches the spine, the energy rises to the crown chakra. We experience a state of openness Hindus call *ananda*, an incomparable joy and happiness inside ourselves, a blissful state that allows us to see the spirit of God as living energy all around us. When the throat chakra opens, spiritual energy passes to the spine. Our words take on deeper meanings. They are connected to higher energy, to the source of life, and we no longer yak away and babble nonsense. People talk to each other, not at each other. They no longer listen to nonsense in their own heads while somebody talks to them. No more than ten percent of conversation penetrates walls of thickness. It's why so many mistakes are made. The real art of conversation has little or nothing to do with what we say. It has to do with how carefully we listen, whether or not we let the external world in, and how we respond to what has been said. When the throat and navel chakras are open, you don't speak from ego need, from tension, anxiety, or fear. You do not have to protect yourself. You speak from a deeper place that permits you to communicate with other human beings.

The chakra directly below the navel is key to meditation practice. It's the center of balance, foundation, and real power in a human being. When we focus the mind in this chakra, when we learn to keep it centered there all the time, the mind becomes a surgical instrument that cuts through tensions deep inside us. The mind opens the foundation of our being. It gives us power that we don't ordinarily live with.

Power by itself is a very dangerous thing, and humility is necessary to counteract its strength. The heart must be open. The easiest way to open the heart is by being grateful. This keeps power in check. But there's no humility, joy, or gratitude in a human being if his heart is closed.

In meditation, we breathe into the heart to strengthen the heart chakra. We feel joy, love, and a very deep sense of gratitude and happiness in the heart. We also relax the throat center, then draw energy through the sex chakra to the base of the spine, up the spine to the top of the head and into the cosmos. The marriage of the human soul and the Higher Soul gives birth to a river of energy that reenters the chakra system of a meditation practitioner. It brings with it knowledge, wisdom, joy, love, gratitude, foundation—higher levels of spiritual practice.

A spiritual life begins when energy recycles itself. The first cycle is simply us learning how to be human. The second cycle of energy brings with it higher consciousness. The energy recycles itself seven times until there's nothing left of us. There's only God.

I teach a simple meditation exercise that transforms all of life's garbage into gold. The hardest part is doing it every day.

Learning to Use the Mind

The energy of mind controls human activity. It's like Medusa's hair going in many directions at the same time. We need to focus it, quiet it, stop its constant chitchat and its nerve-racking voice that keeps us on edge. The mind has all and none of the answers at the same time. It sees a world of opposing factions always in conflict with one another. At the same time, the mind's a great surgical instrument. If focused on the chakra below the navel, it cuts through inner tension and opens our center of balance. Its energy force is strong enough to pierce deep-rooted blocks and tensions. It's simply a matter of whether or not we focus the mind properly.

The journey from the mind to the foundation chakra is one of the longest journeys on Earth, a journey almost impossible to make without discipline and inner strength. It takes years of meditation practice to quiet the mind, to become strong enough to master its chaos—years well-invested if eventually we learn to live day to day with relative peace.

Practitioners of the martial arts are taught to master *chi* — an energy source located in the *hara* (right below the navel) that creates balance and harmony. The power of *chi* will absorb the mind's tensions and proper use of breath helps the practitioner to strengthen the *hara* and develop even more *chi*.

Meditation is similar to the martial arts. Though not exactly self-defense, we learn by meditating how to defend ourselves against conflict and tension. We learn to live on many levels of life at the same time—on Earth, in the cosmos, and outside realms of time and space.

It took me four years to get my mind relatively quiet. This

sounds like a long time, but I've lived with a quiet mind for over thirty-five years now, and four years doesn't seem like such a terrible investment.

Thoughts never completely go away, but I've learned to master them and they no longer control me. I focus my mind's confusion in the *hara*, and bring anger, jealousy, fear, insecurity, guilt, and the rest of the neurotic me into my center of balance. There it gets transformed into energy. The very thing that's killing me gives me life.

All of spiritual work is about getting free of oneself. That's all it has ever been about and all it's about today.

If you want to learn more about chakras, meditation practice is the best way. One can also read books, magazine articles, go to lectures, and study charts, computer programs, and videos, but meditation alone provides direct experience of the chakras. Books introduce us to spiritual possibilities, but no book ever written substitutes for direct experience. You can read them, learn from them, and assimilate facts, which has little or no meaning if the heart is closed, if the mind's noisy, and there's no inner balance. The chakra system becomes another fact filed with millions of other facts that clutter the brain. It's not a system of vital, well-developed centers that connect us to higher energy in the universe. To know chakras exist is not the same as the conscious experience of infinite energy. The written word is not a substitute for a spiritual life. If someone truly wants higher consciousness, they'll find a teacher, then study with that teacher until they master their own inner lives. There's no quicker path; there's no better way to do it.

First we become *human*, a species hard to find on Earth. We no longer have to hide behind our neurosis. Our masks peel off, complacency disappears, and we're no longer angry, fearful, anxiety-ridden, and jealous. We approach the world from a nonjudgmental place within ourselves, a place that accepts the known and unknown, that doesn't have to mold life in our own image. We recognize that to suffer is a unilateral condition, the common denominator that connects human being to human being, a pathway to God and enlightenment. We become empty vessels, then channels for spiritual energy. We learn patience, forgiveness, compassion, and gratitude. No longer filled with egomania and craziness, we can be joyful and loving. We can witness God's

Stuart Perrin

spectacle create and recreate itself every moment of the day. If we're full of tension, there's no room for spirit. There's only so much water you can put in a cup.

The Nature of *Shaktipat*

The guru transmits *shaktipat* (spiritual energy) to help meditation practitioners break down blocks in their chakras and guide them to a deeper inner life. As students of meditation deepen their inner lives and get closer to higher energy, the hands become instruments of healing. They transmit spiritual energy. Often, during intense meditation classes, I'll place my fingers on a student's forehead to draw energy through the chakra system to the top of the head. People fall over, they bounce, jerk, their hands go up in the air, they shout, and pass out. It's a strong practice, but one that decongests ancient blockages in students. Sometimes, during this practice, I think half the class is going to run for the hills. I remember when Rudi would touch my forehead and I'd bounce across the room. He practiced a very advanced and difficult form of meditation impossible to do successfully without great training. It's power can heal people of deep emotional and psychological problems.

The chakra system absorbs only what it's ready to absorb. It's like a sponge. The bigger the system gets, the bigger the sponge becomes and the more energy it can take in. Each time I do hands-on work with meditation practitioners, energy cuts through inner blocks and strengthens their chakra systems. It's a very important part of spiritual work, an important way to transmit teachings.

Centering Yourself

Focus the mind's energy in the chakra below the navel. Then breathe into that chakra and hold the breath for ten seconds. Ask deeply for help to open, to surrender, and to grow spiritually. The will is an important factor. It must be internalized, focused and connected to our need for harmony and balance, and for happy, open lives. When your attention drifts, bring it back. If it drifts again, bring it back again. Bring it back again until you master the mind's flow of energy, until you're no longer the servant of mental and emotional chaos.

It's not easy work. Mostly, we're slaves to mind and emotion. If they go crazy, we go crazy. But with proper meditation training, with mind and emotion focused in the *hara*, we can master inner chaos. Without proper training, human beings are slaves to their own insanity. Until they master mind and emotions, they never live in anything but fog. We must learn techniques of inner work and apply them every day. As I said, it's not easy work, but it is certainly worth the effort.

CHAPTER THREE:

The Spiritual Process

The spiritual process is a day-by-day, step-by-step unfolding of consciousness, a process that breaks down stale and conditioned parts of ourselves to allow rebirth to take place. We're our own worst enemies stuck in stagnant pools of opinion and self-righteousness. We're afraid to let go; we're afraid to step into the unknown; we're afraid to be touched by creative energy.

We live a death-in-life existence that clings to timeworn dogma, to anything familiar, to anything we think represents security on Earth. It's death-in-life that waits impatiently for the end to come, that furtively slips into the minds and hearts of human beings. It's fear that lurks in the human unconscious, fear that paralyzes the minds and hearts of people, that keeps them from tapping a hundred percent of their creative potential. It's an irrational fear linked to death and the unknown, a vise that grips us without mercy, making us angry, sick, unhappy, and unable to escape psychological and emotional prisons.

Once we're free from ourselves, we really are free, but one has to pay a price for freedom of this kind. One has to free himself of preconception, of rightness, of opinions, of the mind that tries to understand life's "Magical Mystery Tour." The spiritual process helps us attain freedom. It breaks down well-insulated realities into component parts. It allows us to rebuild our inner lives, to experience death and rebirth, and to see nature's innate ability to surrender. It's a slow process of evolution of consciousness that unfolds day-by-day, a refinement of density, and a strong desire to get free. Nothing on Earth is in conflict with anything else, and nothing is an end in itself. All things are part of an evolutionary process that gets us closer to God. Only the mind sees conflict; only the mind judges right from wrong.

Without training, spiritual evolution is impossible. One must have discipline, one-pointedness, and, above all, a strong chakra system that can be a vehicle for energy of a higher nature. Meditation teaches us to surrender opposites, to rejoice in the dialectic, to free ourselves of illusion, to no longer accept mirror images of ourselves as reality, and to recognize nothing is bad or good, that no one is better than anyone else. We learn to enjoy the comedy of errors played out before our eyes by bumbling and tumbling people busy going nowhere fast, frightened and childlike, and running headlong into a tenebrous reflection of self. We are not the center of all existence, but our egos latch on like crippled limpets to images we assume are real. Our egos interfere with God-consciousness and with living a spiritual life. They keep us from tapping sources of creative energy nonexistent in ordinary life. Our egos interfere with the whole process of spiritual evolution and attach our consciousness to worldly things. They choose power over gratitude, death over life, material over spiritual, and they wander like buffoons over desolate landscapes filled with reflections from our own minds.

The spiritual process cuts across racial, religious, sexual, and nationalistic borders. It doesn't matter if one's male or female; vegetarian or carnivore; black or white or yellow; Democrat or Republican; Christian, Jewish, Hindu, Buddhist, or Muslim. It doesn't matter what country we inhabit, what city or town or village. All that matters is inner work, and inner work makes us all equal. The rest creates conflict. It separates people from each other, institutionalizes them, gives them a false sense of security and an uneasy peace. It gives them reasons to be angry, to fight, and to lose all sense of their humanity. The heart says, "I am not better than anyone else," but the mind says, "My religion, race, gender, country, or economics makes me superior to other people." The mind turns a human being into a caricature of himself.

Is There an End to All This—a Final Goal?

Yes! Enlightenment. Oneness with God. Rudi compared the spiritual process to an elevator in a department store. He said, "You can get off on any floor and shop." The elevator goes endlessly into the cosmos, but people get distracted shopping for haberdashery, shoes, pots and pans, cosmetics, and thousands of other things more important, in their own minds, than embracing God. Spiritual enlightenment dims in the neon glow of life. It's put on the back burner. We shop for bargains in a material world. Why bother with spiritual lives if the world offers a diversity of drama to fill inner voids?

"The whole idea's to have things and be free of them at the same time," Rudi said to me in his antique shop. "You can't surrender what you haven't experienced. That includes money, relationships, success, power, and whatever else the world offers."

We don't have to live in caves, I thought, while we sat together in his store. We don't have to eat roots, shrubs, and grubs. We do have to embrace life in all its dimensions. At the same time, we have to detach ourselves from whatever life brings our way.

"Sometimes I feel like I'm hacking my way through a jungle with a machete," I said to Rudi. "Welcome to the club," he responded.

"I never know if I'm doing enough, or if I'm doing it right," I said. "That's why we need spiritual teachers," he said. "How else do we know we're still on the path? If we don't ask, our questions go unanswered."

There's a famous Japanese Zen saying: "Climb Mt. Fuji, oh, snail, but slowly, slowly..." It's a very wise metaphor for spiritual work. We mustn't forget it takes time to get to the top of Mt. Fuji. We mustn't rush, but few of us do it a step at a time. Eventually, the snail gets to the top of the mountain, but slowly, step by step, it takes the agonizing journey to the pinnacle of the world. It plods along with timeworn patience; it plods and plods until it gets there.

The real test of spiritual work is to survive ourselves. It has been said, "Many are called, but few are chosen." Millions of people start out on the path, yet, in every generation, only a handful of persistent souls get to its end, but anyone can get there. We all have chakra systems, minds, breath, energy, and will. We have to work at meditation, have endurance, patience, the desire to succeed, and, above everything else, we can't take ourselves for granted. The work should be done joyously and with love. We all want to cut through material and psychological underbrush; we want to overcome our limitations. One day, after we hack for what seems to be a lifetime, we see a little light. At least we're going somewhere, at least we make a conscious effort to grow spiritually. The alternative is to let time pass, to get old and die.

God Hides Behind Masks

God hides behind thousands of masks. He's a master quick-change artist, a magician, vaudeville performer, trickster, wise man, beggar, and fool. He never fits any single role. Like the wind, He changes directions and His legerdemain bewilders the most intelligent of mortals. We can't look for Him. We have to feel Him in our hearts, become one with His being, evolve and grow and see life from a transcendental perspective. If we rekindle childlike innocence, if we feel gratitude and joy in our hearts, then the spectacle of God manifests around us. If not, we bumble along in the underbrush and think darkness is light and light a strange foreboding foray into the unknown. The Earth is a truly special place. Our responsibility is to recognize this simple truth.

The question always is, how do you find the inner child? One has to start with basics, with family, friends, spiritual teachers, the food we eat, the air we breathe, sound, smell, touch, and sight. We start with the most elemental things and then move into more profound subjects. Mostly, we resent our daily activities, our jobs, our parents, brothers, sisters, husbands, wives, and children. We forget why we work. We forget who brought us into the world. We're so caught up in tension that all else disappears. Does it matter if your boss has halitosis, if he's cheap, a schmuck, or a person who bugs you all the time? There are more important reasons to work, such as feeding oneself and one's family. The job teaches us what to do and what not to do. Sometimes the lessons are easy; other times, they are very difficult. But we always learn about ourselves. It's easy to be skeptical; it's easy to find what's wrong with life. It takes an extraordinary person to see the positive in difficult situations.

Every human being does exactly what he or she is supposed to be doing, but most complain about work, relationships, the weather, the place they live, politics, or money. Acceptance of our limitations and ourselves is the first step toward change. We stop beating ourselves up. We use our energy in positive ways. We become the best janitor, waiter, salesman, or taxi driver it's possible to be. It's our time, our lives, and our day. There's no reason to make it miserable; there's no reason to beat ourselves up. Instead, we should be grateful for whatever we are doing for no other reason than gratitude moves something in the heart and allows spiritual energy to enter us. That additional energy moves us to a higher place within ourselves. We find self-worth and dignity, and we value whatever we do. If we can't mop floors with an open heart, we'll never be happy running the household.

The New Year teaches us about death and rebirth. It's a time to remove old coats of paint, to renovate inner living rooms. It's a time to learn from nature's cycle, a time to surrender the old and make room for the new, and a time to recognize life and death are essential to one another. We cling to the past because we're not strong enough to live in the present, but the past is dead. It trails us like a shadow in an empty landscape. We keep looking back. There's no substance, no wisdom, nothing but our distorted point of view of things, nothing but death, pain, and a black hole we've come out of—all a substitute for living in the present.

It takes great strength to live in the moment, to resurrect ourselves from pasts full of guilt, fear, and unhappiness, and enjoy whatever we do. It takes great strength to have three hundred sixty-four "un-birthday" parties, to not get stuck in emotional and psychological mud. We have the right to live wonderful lives, but it's easy to forget this. It's easy to complain about injustice and life's peccadilloes, but life isn't going to change. We have to change. We have to remind ourselves that every day is New Year's. The present doesn't go away. It's always with us. Everything else disappears in the past.

The last time I went to India, I made a pilgrimage to Ramakrishna and Sarada Devi's *samadhi* shrine. While I was in Delhi, an inner voice kept repeating to me, "Go to Calcutta. Go to Calcutta. You have to visit Ramakrishna's *samadhi* shrine." I didn't understand it. I had never been a devotee of Ramakrishna. I knew nothing about his teachings, his person, where he lived, or what his life was like. I knew his name. That's all. I'd seen pictures of him and I knew he'd written a book.

I went to his shrine. I sat in deep meditation before his picture. His voice repeated over and over again, "Drink from the milk of the Mother Goddess...Drink from the milk of the Mother Goddess..." It was a voice that bellowed from deep within myself, a voice demanding that I listen, that I open deeper than I'd ever opened before, a voice that took me to a new cycle in my life.

"The Mother Goddess gives birth to all creation," the voice said. "It's the spectacle of life generating and regenerating itself every moment. If you see this ...if you can witness death and rebirth...if you can live in the moment...that is enlightenment, my son...that is spiritual enlightenment..."

CHAPTER FOUR:

What's Killing You Can Give You Life!

Rudi compared life to an organic garden, a metaphor he used hundreds of times to teach his students to transform tension into creative energy. "Tension is human garbage," he said to me in his store one day. "It needs to be broken down into compost that feeds our inner soil. If we don't break down our tension, it destroys us."

He took a large bite out of life, chewed it, swallowed it, digested it, shit out what he didn't need, and then transformed the rest into energy. "You need to be a warrior," he continued, "a perfectly balanced samurai in the heart of battle, a happy samurai, a slightly mad samurai, a samurai in tune with both life and death."

The external world is more of a dream than the dreams we have in our sleep. We bumble around like blind fools in a labyrinthine maze created by our mind. We're logical to the point of absurdity. Every time we think we understand something, the universe gives us a swift kick in the butt. It cripples us with its own brand of logic. We struggle with it. We try to make sense out of nonsense; we drive ourselves crazy with well-worked-out and plausible schemes. It's a "Divine Comedy," but more often a treacherous tightrope walk we take on life's stage. People never learn. They believe they know what's right. They keep bumping into other righteous people like toy cars bump into each other at a carnival.

Rudi once said, "You've got to put compost in the earth or it'll stink. What's in the earth bears fruit. What's outside the earth smells, rots, breeds disease and stagnation."

Tension fuels the soul force of every human being, but first it needs to be transformed into *chi*. If it remains in the mind and heart, we experience conflict, lack of balance, lopsidedness, and we're incapable of dealing with opposing forces. There's no foundation inside us. We use about five percent of our creative capacity. We're tired, unhappy, always complaining, and always fighting with the world and ourselves.

The word "transformation" is big in pop culture today. We read about it in every new age magazine, but, from the act of reading about it to the moment we can effectively transform tension into spiritual energy, therein lies a chasm difficult to cross. Information gleaned from books and periodicals can work against us if we don't build strong chakra systems. They clutter the mind and give us reason to pontificate to a "why me?" generation of complainers, to little Mary Poppinses in combat boots, to sugar-plum fairies and Tinkerbells that flit about in the dark night of the human soul. Information does little or nothing to rid us of obstacles lodged deep within us.

Why Am I the Only One Who Suffers?

One moment it's spring, the next winter, summer, or fall. Each moment is different. Each moment teaches us something new about life. We believe spring breezes are better than winter snowstorms, but the Earth's ecology demands both. If there are no monsoons in Southeast Asia, the glaciers in Canada and the North Pole will melt. The world's ecology would be in lots of trouble. Life's a multifaceted hodgepodge of subtle changes. We can't expect it to be only one way; we can't expect to walk between the raindrops.

"We're always wondering, "Why me? Why am I the only one on Earth who suffers?" We're blind to the fact that suffering is pandemic. It crosses every border. It cares little for race, religion, or nationality. No one escapes it, yet everyone wonders, "Why me?" Rarely, if ever, do people use their suffering to get to God. They lament, pray, prostrate themselves, cry, and bemoan their fates, but almost never use suffering as a tool to grow. Things will always get rough, winter will always come, but, so what? Winter reminds us to wait patiently for spring.

Nature is a great teacher. It moves through cycles of death and rebirth without regret, without attachment, with *noblesse oblige*, a pure spirit that regenerates itself over and over again. It beckons man to learn its simple lessons of life and truth. Nature doesn't bother itself with mind and logic. It doesn't have to understand anything. It is—that's all, nothing more, nothing less. It doesn't have to be anything, and it doesn't have to become anything.

Nature is our best example of the Universal Soul's closeness to God. When a storm disrupts the peace of heaven and Earth, there are dark clouds, thunder, lightning, and a sudden downpour of heavy rain. The rivers overflow and streets are flooded. All havoc breaks loose. A moment later, the clouds part, the sun comes out, the sky is blue, and rays of sunlight sparkle in pools of water on the streets. Nature has no memory of storms, no memory of dark clouds and turbulence. It moves on to the next beat, the next rhythm, the next moment in time and space.

People cling to old pain like limpets cling to coral. They refuse to let go. It's as if old pain's a good excuse to destroy the present. Why live now if the past was so painful? Why let go and enjoy the moment? Nature doesn't have problems with memory. Neither the past nor future exists in nature's consciousness. It's not a storehouse filled with guilt, anxiety, fear, revenge, and anger. It takes life a day at a time. Therein lies a great teaching. How many human beings can take life a day at a time? Not many. Most are trapped in the past and the future. Most are crippled by a mind that wanders.

The past no longer exists and the future is the present unfolding itself, but the mind's turbulence drifts from past to present to future without a moment's lapse. The mind has its own agenda. It could care less that the moment's changed, that clouds have parted, that the sun is out. It clings to old memories and refuses to let go of them. It refuses to witness God's spectacle on Earth, to take each moment as it comes, and let life be.

Human beings serve the mind. They listen to and obey its quirky orders and follow its limited wisdom into tenebrous voids within themselves. They're torn apart by conflicting thoughts, by powerful fears, and addled voices that fill a hazy landscape in the brain. They've lost touch with the ebb and flow of life and death that moves through history and time. There's little joy, little gratitude; there are mostly loud decibels of inner noise that replace love. So we turn to doctors, psychiatrists, and psychologists for answers to problems these professionals have yet to resolve for themselves. We worship pop-culture idols—the Rambos with twenty-million-dollar pectorals that pop off the movie screen, the whole demented lust for power and money and its idiotic voice that screams louder than silent inner voices of spiritual seekers; the upside down moral code of power-crazed moguls, the whole moth-eaten rigmarole that torments human spirit—with nothing to do, with nowhere to go. Modern man listens to this madness and believes it's worth pursuing. Modern man talks so intelligently about nonsense and seeks to elevate mediocrity to godlike status.

We are the problem. We're also the solution. To resolve the problem, we need to work on ourselves; we need to turn off the mind's voice box; we need to observe nature's nobility; and we need to be grateful for little things.

The ego's diseased infrastructure keeps us from ever having clear vision in life. I know life is hard, but, so what! We all need roughage. If we don't have roughage in our diet, our digestive systems get messed up. We'd never go to the toilet. Life's difficulty is part of a healthy diet. It can be used to grow. It can be transformed into positive energy. You just have to know how to do it. You have to get proper training.

People say, "Kundalini yoga is dangerous." It's important to have a meditation teacher who knows how the spiritual process works, who's walked the path, and who's willing to guide you to the other side of yourself.

A teacher has to give away his teachings. If not, he or she will never attain spiritual enlightenment. A teacher dreams of a great student, of someone hungry enough to pay the price for growth and higher consciousness. He needs a great disciple as much as the disciple needs him. It's a marriage based on divine will, a marriage performed by God because both teacher and disciple are ready for each other. Neither is more important. Both fulfill their roles in the evolutionary process; both are ready to become one with God.

In the Old Testament, there's a section in which so-and-so bequeaths so-and-so, and for page after page we follow the lineage from Adam and Eve down. Spiritual work is similarly passed on from generation to generation in a never-ending process of evolution.

Yet people are skeptical when it comes to gurus, and rightfully so. Many gurus use persona, ego, magical gifts and powers to control unwary students. They make huge sums of money, covet power, and create slaves out of people with weaker egos. They can be very dangerous. They're minor-league kings without hearts or wisdom. They're dogmatists and often tyrants. Seekers beware the bleak light that emanates from power-crazed spiritual zealots.

The marriage of disciple and teacher is different. It has nothing to do with throngs of people, with groups and temples and prayers and devotional outpourings of love; it has nothing to do with diets and fads and who and what we worship; it has nothing to do with mind or anything the mind understands. It's a marriage performed by God, a marriage based on surrender, on mutual work between teacher and disciple, on mutual need to be spiritually enlightened. It's a marriage so sacred it forces both parties to surrender ego, mind, opinions, thoughts on right or wrong. It forces both parties to evolve and grow closer to God, to pay any price for their enlightenment. It's been written, "Many are called and few are chosen." Those few who are *chosen* must live in the light of a spiritual marriage.

Why Wallow in Garbage?

It's not necessary to know the details and history of our neurosis and problems. Why wallow in garbage? Just throw it out. Get rid of the stink. When demolitionists tear down a building, they don't examine each brick. They dynamite the building, it collapses, then they clear the rubble and cart it away. A new building is built on the same spot. Ego is an old wreck of a building; breath and mind are like dynamite blasts that blow up its foundation. If we grind ego into nothingness, we're left with room within ourselves for spiritual energy. We've taken a large step towards working out our karma.

Life's not going to hurt us any more than it's already hurt us. Somehow, we've all survived. When I was twenty, I worried about the future. Now that I'm older and I've survived the "future,"

I have to laugh when I think about all the energy wasted over nothing. It's just as easy for people to use that same energy to build a strong spiritual life. It's so much better to trust life. It's so much better to open our hearts and enjoy the moment. Whatever happened to us in the past has made it possible for us to be in the present. What else matters? Being angry, upset, clinging to old karma, holding on to phantoms, to what once was, to what people did to us—it's better to forgive, to move on, and to learn to live in the present.

I'm grateful for every single thing that's ever happened to me: good, bad, joyous, painful, whatever. I'm a product of all that. To hate people in my past is to hate myself. I can't be caught up in what happened to me. I live in this moment and nothing else matters. If I die, it's all over. There's nothing more to worry about, no more financial and relationship problems. I can take a rest from a meddlesome mind, but death isn't the solution. Living in the moment, trusting myself and God, feeling self-worth and love, joy, clarity, open heartedness—these are solutions to life-long problems.

I don't have to work through past issues. I've already lived them. Why reincarnate phantoms from a fuzzy world?

If we were abused as children, why continue to abuse ourselves today? Once was enough. We don't have to spend the rest of our lives reliving the horror of the past, reliving dramas created by the mind to unhinge the present, a mind that clings to self righteousness, that can't forgive, that can't let go of anger; a mind that makes us suffer over and over again for sins of the father, for lack of consciousness of the mother, a mind that stunts our growth, that creates forty-year-old mental and emotional Lilliputians. It's not necessary to remember what happened in our childhood, but it's important to transform past trauma into spiritual energy, to free ourselves from phantoms that haunt the unconscious, to learn to love ourselves, our parents, our children, and to stop being victims of other people's lack of consciousness. It's important to build a strong chakra system and use the mind and breath to transform garbage into gold.

CHAPTER FIVE:

The Rhythm of Life

The heart's rhythm is the rhythm of life, a rhythm that beats twenty-four hours a day non-stop for eternity. The mind and emotions interfere with the heart's natural rhythm. They create manic-depressive states that throw the heart out of sync. They bounce human beings, like Ping-Pong balls, between elation and depression, rarely, if ever do they let the heart's natural rhythm attune itself to the rhythm of the universe.

I've yet to meet a human being who's normal. We all have problems. Without them, the Earth would be a boring, terribly uninteresting place to live, a cabbage patch, a parched desert, a veritable wasteland of human inactivity. Billions of crazy people play roles in a divine comedy that's called life. Each person's a unique entity unto himself, with ideas, opinions, and thoughts on right and wrong. Each person's energy is not only off-kilter but also a part of the design of the universe. Therein lies the "rub."

It's okay to be slightly crazy, to be different, to be a fool in a world full of so-called opinionated people. There is nothing wrong with that. It's okay to be unique, especially in a world in which it's impossible to find normalcy. The question is: What do we do with our uniqueness? Do we use it to destroy other people, to destroy ourselves, or to grow spiritually? Do we live like human beings or like animals? Do we blame life for our problems, or work on ourselves to resolve them? Life is never going to be easy. If we accept that, and not mope around like disgruntled porkers, we'll embrace problems and the creativity they inspire; we'll be grateful for them because they make us work on ourselves. The first step is

to learn to trust ourselves; then we can trust the rest of the world.
Jealousy's a sickness rooted deep in the heart. The jealous torture themselves more than the victims of their jealousy. We have
to feel compassion and forgiveness for them. No one can hurt
us unless we let them, not if we open our hearts, feel love, joy,
forgiveness, and the rest of the higher emotions. It's a different
kind of logic, one that trusts the world, that trusts ourselves, that
sees God's spectacle manifesting in everything around us. It takes
a very strong person to live with trust. It requires powerful *chi*,
balance, and foundation. Without them, innocence is demol-
ished by life. It can't withstand roughage. It's like a child without
parents, a child that needs guidance and strength to teach it the
ways of the world.

I've noticed that any positive experience in my life is always followed by a negative experience. The same is true of negative experiences. Elation becomes depression in split seconds depending
on what happens to us. We're like manic-depressive wind-up toys
that bang into sordid reflections of ourselves. We believe knights
on white horses will sweep us away into magical kingdoms. Pain
and suffering will go away. Alice will sleep forever in Wonderland.
But the moment changes. Good and evil then dance to a scratchy
tune on a broken record. One dissolves into the other. Eventually
we can't tell the difference.

I can never remember it being any different, not in my childhood, teenage years, twenties, or thirties. There was always the
battle of polar opposites that consumed every moment of my time.
Always, goodness was followed by evil. So, when good things
happen, I stay detached; when negative things happen, I still
remained detached. I've seen "The Good" put on demon masks
and spit fire in my face; I've used negative experiences as steps
on a ladder that leads to profound spiritual growth. I try not to
exhaust my energy when good things happen. If I make a lot of
money, if my relationship is going well, if the sun's out and it's a
balmy day, it's better to stay quiet, remain detached, and have no
expectations. There is no telling what the next moment will bring,
no telling when the winds will change. It's hard to learn this. We
expect the world to be a certain way.

The mind creates its own realities, and we step into that reality
thinking everyone else sees the world like we do. We're children

adrift in an adventure comic book, in a landscape fabricated from thought. We're unsure of ourselves, nervous, trying to find the errant knight who's going to joust with the windmill. Nothing is good and nothing is bad. It's all a hodgepodge of mind and emotion. When things go wrong, we whine like brats on a street corner and scream because mommy doesn't want to buy us an ice cream cone. We forget the world doesn't work the exact way we think it should. There are billions of people on Earth. Every one of them sees a different reality. Somewhere along the way, there needs to be compromise. Each of us needs to be patient. If one thing doesn't work, there's always the next, and the next, and the next. Then, we live our lives in step with an inner rhythm. The heart dictates actions, and we no longer battle with right and wrong.

Meditation teaches us to reverse a lifetime of bad toilet training. Our parents never tell us, "Focus your mind below the navel, strengthen your *chi*, learn inner balance, open the heart chakra, and quiet the mind." For the most part, our parents don't understand spiritual training. We're brought up to believe happiness comes from the outside—marriage, boyfriends, girlfriends, money, a house in the suburbs, a car, a refrigerator, etc. If it were that easy, there'd be more happy people on Earth. But happiness, like an elusive butterfly, lives at the center of the human heart, a heart that needs to be opened, reopened, strengthened, and filled with spiritual energy. Once we learn to be happy, we've learned everything there is to learn on Earth.

I went to the country one day to look at a house for sale, a beautiful house in a charming town near the Hudson River.

"You can make an offer," the real estate agent said to me.

"How much?" I asked.

She quoted a reasonable price, so I left a bid. Three days later, *Architectural Digest* did an article on the house. The price went up $400,000.

"What to do?" I thought. "There's no reason to get crazy. Wait and see what happens after the fanfare is over. I could rant and rave and plot to blow up the *Architectural Digest* office. But it's just a house. If the hoopla fades, I'll talk to the owner. If he hasn't sold it, the price will probably go down. Life's too short to get crazy about a house. If I trust my inner voice, it'll guide me to the right place, it'll make sure I choose whatever I need to evolve spiritually. It'll even lead me to the right house."

As much as I liked the house, I knew life's ever-changing rhythms would force me to surrender what I like and dislike. I knew the subtleties of change transcend human comprehension. "It's impossible to do everything we like," I thought. "We must learn to detach ourselves from situations and make room for God to send us what we're supposed to have." So I surrendered the house. A year later, I purchased another house in Woodstock that was much more beautiful, less expensive, and more to my taste.

Nothing works out exactly as we plot it in our minds. Life's rhythms change each moment. If we miss a beat, we lose sight of the creative process, of miracles that manifest the next moment, of real answers to our questions.

Make Room for Spiritual Growth

Real spiritual work does not cultivate expectations. It takes life a moment at a time. It gives us strength to flow with changes. One day life is paradise on Earth; the next day, heaven becomes hell and the human mind struggles to figure out what happened. Nothing special happened. Energy manifests as polar opposites. But we have expectations. No matter how many times we've voyaged through hell, we complain about it; we believe life is *supposed* to be different. We can't figure why we suffer. But the dialectic does not disappear, not until we recognize there is no positive or negative. There's only energy. Positive and negative are the same character in different costumes. We've got to use them both to grow spiritually.

I remember the pain in Rudi's eyes when blocks in him broke down to make room for spiritual growth. Then, two hours later, he'd be like a child, his eyes full of sweetness and love, his heart aglow, joy flowed from every muscle and cell in his body. He never begrudged the pain. He knew how to use it consciously. He learned through years of meditation practice that death and rebirth are essential to inner development. It's the cost of a spiritual life. It's better to go through the grinder consciously than unconsciously. At least we can use pain to get closer to God. We suffer anyway, so why not use suffering for spiritual growth, why not work to the other side of oneself and into the domain of higher energy in the universe? There's a child in us that wants to be born, a child nestled in the womb of transcendental consciousness. He awaits us. He wants to embrace us, to share love and joy with us. We are that child. We just have to find him.

None of us is perfect. We'll have problems until the day we die. Since perfection's the domain of God and His angels and madmen, inner growth is the best we mortals can do. We evolve closer to perfection. We struggle with Jacob's angel as we climb a ladder to heaven. Our problems are reminders that we're not perfect; we have to work on ourselves; we can't take ourselves for granted. We're creatures of necessity. Without it, the world would be a stagnant pool of water, a musty, dusty, crusty barnacle on the butt of a clown. We have to do whatever we can to free ourselves from ourselves. No judgment, no dogma, and no opinion, wise or otherwise, should interfere with the growth process. The mind will only get in the way. You do what you have to do to get to God. That's it! The rest delays the process of evolution.

The human heart is a very difficult and touchy place. Its energy shifts and changes like wind on an open plain. We need gratitude to master its subtle changing landscape. If the heart is the seat of love, and love, by its very nature, defines the evolution of mankind, the more open the heart, the more evolved the person, and the closer they are to happiness. It takes years to get the heart open, to rediscover the child in oneself, and give it the freedom to live. The mind doesn't trust. It analyzes. It figures life out. It's skeptical about most things it doesn't understand. But if the heart's open, then trust is possible and cynicism disappears. If trust becomes a formidable ally in the struggle to evolve, we embrace life and are no longer afraid to express our deepest feelings.

These are not easy lessons. People view evolution ass backwards. They base it on intellectual discovery, information, and technical advancement, but never on the heart, never on joyful sharing of love, happiness, and inner well-being. Computers do not bring happiness. They bring information, money, and power, none of which constitutes highly-evolved goals. A person born into a family worth billions of dollars isn't necessarily happier than a person born into difficult economic circumstances. They might be richer, but, so what? If there's no gratitude, if they're blinded by wealth, if position and power mean more than humility, they've flunked the test. The only successful people on Earth are happy people. The rest of humanity's got to repeat the course.

Living with Higher Energy

People today all want to do "their own thing." It's a slightly mad, egoistic step into illusion because their "thing" lodges in confused, often megalomaniacal, minds that twist the image of the world into a reflection of itself. I could never figure out what my "thing" is. I don't understand anything that goes on in my life. I trust spiritual energy. It does a much better job of running my life than I do. I'm grateful to get up in the morning, do the day, and take care of each "thing" as it comes along. There's no shortage of creative energy. There's only my limitation, my inability to grasp the subtleties of God's universe. I'm not afraid to admit this. I'd rather struggle with my limitations than crystallize in academic portraits of myself. The day I arrive full force in the precincts of "my thing" is the day my life's over. My mind will control every activity. I'll serve my ego, my will, and my righteousness. I'll jam up the learning process, deny myself new experiences, lock myself in a prison, and pass the day looking fearfully into the eye of my own "thing."

As a young man, my "thing" nearly killed me. I wanted to be a writer. I worked at it twelve hours a day. Obsessed with literature, art, and music, confused and unhappy, my "thing" controlled me like a demonic god. One day, Rudi told me to burn all my manuscripts. I tearfully burned them. I surrendered my writing and didn't go back to it for ten years. When I wrote again, it no longer consumed me. Instead of being an obsession, it became one more creative outlet among many that made up my life.

Human beings are obsessive-compulsive creatures caught in whirlpools of misguided energy. They lack detachment. Their habits consume them whole. There's little or no spiritual training to keep compulsive natures in balance, little understanding of the adage "less is more." They live way beyond their limits and exhaust their wellspring of creative energy. There's no trust of God, no conscious refinement of neurotic states of being. Belief in higher energy is useless if that belief system is locked in the mind. One spends one's life waiting for Samuel Beckett's Godot. People turn into flayed images of themselves. There's nothing but mind waging war against itself. We have to make higher energy an organic part of our inner lives. To believe in God and rot away in that belief is a useless trap. If there's nothing open in a human being, if he's more desert than oasis, if he's like rotten fruit, if his voice cries out from the past and tries hard to make statements in the present, he lives in a theater of the absurd where the dead mimic live people in a loud dumb-show staged in life's ever-evolving sanatorium. It's one thing to talk about a spiritual life, another to make it fundamental to everyday existence, to make ideas into reality. Then we must do what's necessary to have a spiritual life. There are no longer excuses. We lay them to rest. We take full responsibility for day-to-day growth. We become spiritual warriors.

It's easy to keep one's heart open when good times are here, but nobility of soul is found in people who keep their hearts open during bad times. They do not make distinctions. They've discovered good and bad are creations of the mind. There are only life's myriad manifestations. Each is a test, and we have to survive it. Can we find love, joy, sweetness, and gratitude in the dark night of the human soul? That's a true test of our connection with God. When well-planned excursions into the unknown break down and all that's left are fragments of ego lying at our feet—*maya*, broken dreams, a dead end built from patches of thought and emotion, a grand illusion, limbo—these are prefaces to spiritual spring cleaning.

Cleaning up *maya* is a priority. But the razzle-dazzle of illusion perplexes the human brain. It's like flashing neon lights in Times Square. The attraction's great, but behind it all, there's little or no substance: the same old movie, a not-so-good Broadway play, a mediocre restaurant that sells passably bland food to tourists that covet Day-Glo turn-on stories to tell friends back home in America's heartland. We deceive ourselves with bright lights and loud music. We forget inner well-being, silence, and a dialogue with infinite energy in the universe—simple truths that speak to us beneath the noise of the crowd. Time and again, we play into the hands of *maya*'s not-so-subtle con. We settle for illusion as a way of life and rarely, if ever, turn inwards and root ourselves in silence.

Listening

Listening is an art form learned after years of meditation practice. Most people are so busy carrying on conversations with themselves that they haven't time to listen to anyone else. Mental noise has deadened their eardrums, nervous systems, and their ability to sustain conversation. They can't hear their own inner voice. Dialogue with friends, relatives, and strangers sounds more like static on a radio than words chosen to communicate needs. People are so wrapped up in thought, fear, insecurity, and the rest of life's assorted pressures that the inner voice of silence is drowned in the uproar. People rarely, if ever, say what they mean. They talk for the sake of talking. Their words are bandied about on the surface of life and most conversation fades into the great yawn of memory. Little or nothing has meaning in the present, little or nothing is remembered an hour or two later. Most conversation is a cacophony made unbearable by people's desperate need to communicate nonsense. Their talk is very cheap background music to the soap opera played out by human beings every day. No one really listens to anyone else. They're too busy listening to their own convoluted thoughts.

Listening is the key to intelligent conversation. Our words mean nothing if we just respond to our own thoughts, if we haven't heard what the other person says to us, if we talk through the mind's static, through a self-indulgent need to impose our reality on someone else. How's it possible to communicate if there's no clarity within ourselves, if we struggle every day with insecurity, with righteousness, with a host of other egomaniacal noisemakers that clutter our brain?

Within every person there's a voice that guides him or her to higher levels of consciousness, a voice that speaks from the heart. We have to learn to trust it. It's our teacher. It guides us through the labyrinthine maze of daily living. In time, we learn to listen to voices deep within ourselves, to trust them and to find self-worth and joy in our hearts. It teaches us to listen to other people with compassion, love, willingness to share our lives, and with patience. It teaches us to listen to silence on the other side of the din, to trust both silence and our intuition. Time waits for us to get to the other side of the noise that congests our minds and emotions.

We have to learn to trust life. Distrust creates dark inner rhythms that confuse life's purpose—a closed heart, an analytical and skeptical view of things, depression, sadness, neurosis, and an inability to love. We isolate ourselves in self-righteousness. The more intelligent we are, the greater our isolation, the more perceptive our view of life's injustices, and the more afraid we are of being hurt. It's a thick veneer worn by neurotic children in adult bodies, children too frightened to open their hearts and listen to deeper rhythms. The mind is enough for them. Its cold, dry, logical approach to life systematically drains juice from the heart. If we distrust anything, it should be our mind because it has all the answers. Beneath its noise is the voice of silence. If we trust silence, it guides us to a place connected to higher energy in the universe; it gives us the strength to resolve our problems. The principle is easy, but doing it is very difficult.

Patience as a Teacher

Patience is another art we have to learn, first with ourselves, then with other people. We are fallible, mistake-ridden creatures that bumble through life like drunken dogs that bay at the moon, never happy with our lot, we find fault, judge and criticize other people. We're full of guilt and fear, and we lack certitude. It's difficult for us to accept our own mistakes and to forgive other people for theirs. We forget that no one succeeds in life without making hundreds of mistakes. They teach us to change and to move on.

Patience teaches us to be grateful for difficult situations. Each of us can graph our positive and negative experiences, a graph full of highs and lows by learning to be patient and to have gratitude. It's easy to be grateful after winning the lottery, but gratitude for lessons learned while taking out the garbage...therein lies nobility of soul. A human being can free himself of highs and lows by learning patience and gratitude.

Most financial woes are self-induced indulgences used by people to emotionally and mentally cripple themselves. They are rarely, if ever, relative to the human condition. This might sound strange, but spend ten minutes in Calcutta. You'll discover real financial woe. The poverty is mind-boggling, almost surreal.

Most financial need should be basic. Can we feed ourselves, pay the rent, buy clothing, and take care of our families? Everything else is gravy. But we make everything else a priority. We become gluttons to our own greed. We forget how simple life can be; we forget to be grateful for the food God puts on our table.

We waste too much energy on complaints about life's injustices, energy that could be used to take care of difficult situations, which could help us to see things more clearly and make better choices. Inner silence helps to clear up problems. It transforms them into *chi* and makes us realize there's something higher in the universe than mind and ego. It takes us to the next level in our spiritual evolution. If the mind and emotions are quiet, we can then make conscious choices. We're not blinded by confusion. We have energy enough to find balance and harmony in life. We can apply that energy to economic well-being, to relationships, to being happy, joyous, grounded human beings no longer at war with ourselves and with others.

There's layer upon layer of emotional and mental bedrock between higher consciousness and ourselves. Though the surface crust erodes and disintegrates, though it changes constantly and resembles a dream, we must see it for what it is: *maya*, illusion, a universe that shifts and changes and is mostly a projection of human mind — a pickpocket of a universe that steals the soul of mankind. If we don't trust the voice in our heart, if we don't listen to the dialogue between God and ourselves, then we're stuck with a mirror image of mind: a half-crazed and noisy reality that reflects the confused inner state of a human being, a lack of balance, and a delusional search for self in a dreamlike world that has no substance. There's no easy way. It takes work and more work to blast inner bedrock, to free ourselves from ourselves so we can move along the path to spiritual enlightenment.

The breath and mind are tools of meditation that guides us to pockets of "spiritual oil" deep in the unconscious, to a place of renewal, of rebirth, to a transcendental view of the world around us. The breath and mind help us get past ourselves. We are the problem, yesterday, today, and tomorrow; we are the problem, and we'll always be the problem. We are also the solution to the problem, but a solution not to be found in logical well-worked-out theories created by mind, not to be found in ritual or religion, or in dogmatic principles, or in ancient or modern treatises on God and the nature of God. The solution is an experiential one. It's in day-by-day meditation work to penetrate vast resources of energy in the unconscious, to use mind and breath to open chakras and to nurture our entire inner being with spirit. It doesn't matter what technique is used, as long as it works, as long as it clears the obstacles between oneself and higher consciousness.

Gandhi Politics

It's difficult for people to keep their mouths shut. They're jealous, opinionated, vociferous, and insecure, and they project negativity in the direction of family, friends, associates in the work place, and life in general. Everybody has opinions. It we listen to them, they disrupt inner harmony and well-being. They make us doubt ourselves, our paths, and the connection we have with higher energy in the universe. Secure persons are never jealous of other people's successes. They wish everyone well. They compete with no one. People's opinions mean nothing to them. They can swim with sharks without being devoured by them.

Only insecure people put others down. Only sick minds and hearts revel in misfortune, failure, and human misery. It takes years of inner work to develop real security. It takes years to conquer jealousy, pettiness, smallness of mind and opinion, to sincerely wish people wonderful lives, to remain unruffled when gossip's flung at our feet, to believe in ourselves, to respect every religion and denomination, and not for a moment believe our lives are more important than the lives of others.

In the early 1970's, Rudi had asked me to teach meditation at an Ashram he established in Denton,Texas. The center prospered both spiritually and economically. Many students came to study there, businesses developed, and people worked together to build a strong and healthy situation. It was in the mid-seventies, about four years after Rudi's death, when a friend of mine telephoned me early one Monday morning, and told me the head of the Denton Baptist Church, in his Sunday morning sermon, announced in a loud and commanding voice: *The devil lives in the Ashram*. There were over three thousand people in the congregation. Instantly, I had visions of white-robed and hooded Ku Klux Klan members burning crosses on my front lawn. Denton had redneck groups that lived in and around its precincts. "The head of the Baptist church is a powerful man," I thought. "He influences a lot of people." I needed an answer. After fifteen minutes, or more, of deep meditation, I opened my eyes and looked out the window of my antique store. A flower shop was across the street. "That's the answer," I said to myself. I bought a large bouquet of flowers and sent it to the head of the Baptist church. I enclosed a letter that outlined projects undertaken by members of the Ashram. In the letter I stated how we had helped get hundreds of young people off drugs, how we taught in prisons, hospitals, reform schools, and halfway houses, and how we ran businesses to support ourselves and in every way tried to be an asset to the community. "If you really want to find out what goes on at the Ashram," I wrote at the conclusion of the letter, "you have an open invitation to have dinner with us at our house."

About a month later, I received a letter of apology from the minister. He said to me, "Dear Mr. Perrin, I just want you to know that I'm sorry I gave my talk. I'll never do it again. I really didn't know what went on in your situation. I've found out you've done more good for this community than most any other group in the area. Please accept my apology."

"Gandhi politics," I thought as I took a sigh of relief. "The politics of love saved the day."

Most opinions lack substance. They're founded on hearsay and they justify a sick need to put people down. No matter who we are in this life, there'll always be someone with an opinion about us; there'll always be someone who's going to have negative things to say. We can't escape it. There are just too many mosquitoes on Earth. We just have to detach ourselves from opinion, get strong, feel our own self-worth, and not worry about rumor's endless hiss. Most of us have no idea what to do with opinion. We let it get into our thoughts, we fight with it, hide from it, and, in many cases, we're destroyed by it. The lives of saints are generally flush with religious opinion. Their critics thought them to be mad; their proponents heralded miraculous acts. They were crucified and tortured in God's name, and they never, not for a moment, wavered in their beliefs. The real battlefield of truth is our struggle to free ourselves from prisons we create for ourselves.

We don't get free when we fight other people; we just prevent ourselves from finding the truth and obstruct the path to spiritual enlightenment. We blame others for our own limitations, but the real battlefield exists within each and every one of us. There, we struggle to free ourselves from deep-rooted obsessions that pinion us to Earth, obsessions that drive us crazy. Therein lies the true battlefield where the self is up against its own strange nature. It's a fifteen-round heavyweight bout, a toe-to-toe slugfest of ego versus spirit, mind versus heart, balance versus imbalance, clarity versus vagueness, life versus death—a slugfest that pits the human need for spiritual enlightenment against lesser, more apparent goals that consume our time and energy.

CHAPTER SIX:

Work and a Spiritual Life

Work is an important determination of spiritual growth, not the particular job we do nor the business we run, but our ability to work at a high level no matter what form the work takes. We should be grateful for work and perfect the work until we master it. There's no work to be ashamed of. It all contributes to life's design. It all demands that we grow and change and use creative energy to absorb pressure on the job.

We spend a good portion of our day at work. It's easy to belittle jobs, to berate ourselves, and to complain about low salaries, benefits, and working conditions. In truth, labor-management struggles can be hell. People enslave each other in low-paying jobs that transform human beings into insects. But it's still our time, our lives, and we can bitch and complain, or we can find reasons to be grateful. Our lives should be full of wonder. Just the act of breathing is a miracle, the act of eating, sleeping, walking, talking—it's all a miracle of God. Like William Blake once said, "Everything that lives is holy." A job site is a place to learn about ourselves, to become more conscious of who or what we are, to refine our abilities and use them the best we can on Earth.

Necessity forces us to be active in the world, and ambition helps make our lives successful. Many people lack ambition. They're afraid of success, responsibility, pressure, the lure of money, of making mistakes, of no longer using failure as an excuse for their miserable lives.

There's no sense paralyzing oneself with fear. We have to step into the unknown anyway, take risks, and shoulder life's responsibilities. We have to get up every morning and greet the day. So, why not take a chance? Why not let ambition guide us to successful lives?

"Business creates pressure, and responsibility and pressure makes me go deeper within myself," Rudi once said. "A diamond is the product of millions of years of pressure." Human beings who thrive under pressure have learned to detach their minds and emotions from events. They stay centered, focused, and balanced. They're able to see clearly what needs to be done.

I never wanted to be a billionaire, but I find business pressures healthy. They remind me to sit down every day and meditate. The alternative is scary. People are blinded by the glitter of money. They chase it with a passion that becomes unhinged. Greed takes over. Money is the sole god to be worshipped. It must be obtained at any cost to life, limb, and happiness. Pressure forces me to go deep inside myself and meditation helps me to regenerate energy lost in the business world. There's no other way I can deal with it. It's a way I've found to keep myself from going crazy.

Money is just energy; it's a provider of life and a way to care for one's well-being. It also scares many people. They have to cross into the unknown and actively pursue success. They have to make their lives work. They have to step out of the shadows, free themselves from fear and insecurity, and take on greater responsibility.

Ambition releases torrents of tension that sweep us away in emotional and psychological tides, that often washes us out to sea. It can also guide us to spirit. It all depends on how we use it or how it uses us. If the only successful person on Earth is a happy person, the rest of humanity grovels in minefields of tension. The rest of humanity is a prisoner of ambition or the lack thereof.

Success and Failure

We must learn that success and failure are one and the same energy. Both are prisons if they become ends in themselves. Both eat away our minds and hearts, and both cause endless pain, suffering, and disease. Either can kill us, or drive us mad, or remind us that life's a dream we float around in like aberrated figures in a Magritte painting.

No one succeeds in life without experiencing failure. One attracts the other. People afraid to fail insulate ambition in bubbles created by the mind. They live in personal petrified forests, in little worlds of self-inflicted perfection, frightened worlds that border the unknown. They never take a chance. They see life's conflicts as a threat to their own security, a stagnant security created from threads of fear. Ambition attracts success and failure. It keeps us from solidifying. It forces us to sally forth in life's adventure, to travel the economic Mirkwood, to slay dragons, griffins, and motley monsters, to find the pot of gold or the damsel in distress. In truth, there is no such thing as failure. There are only mistakes. We need to learn from them and go on.

There's no guarantee we're going to succeed in life. We have to take each day at a time and measure our self-worth by the amount of openness in our hearts, by our mastery of tension, and by our ability to live quietly in the moment. We can't compare ourselves with other people. There's no sense in it. No matter how successful we become, there's always someone more successful. There are no guarantees that concern success. There's only life's divergent river and it converges in a great ocean called death. No earthly ambition can conquer death. It's the great equalizer. It reduces everything to a seven-foot piece of turf, to a box full of ashes, to nothingness, to total surrender.

Death in life is worse than dying at the end of life. Its stagnant pool attracts every kind of vermin and disease. It forces us to pay for life unconsciously. We suffer without knowing why we suffer. We don't know where to turn, but our pain intensifies, it controls all our activity; it reduces life to a distorted reflection of our former selves. The psychic muscle system (chakras) dries up and we use only five percent of our creative potential. It's death in life, a state of being more hideous than failure.

Goals are important, but they aren't ends in themselves. They motivate us to work and grow and move toward better life situations. They stimulate our minds and emotions, keep our energy moving, and teach us about obstacles and hurdles. Once we attain our goal, we too often lose ambition. We're tired of climbing the ladder. We'd rather wallow in our success. We have money, fame, and power. Why continue to chase higher goals? Why be a glutton? It's easy to become satisfied with ourselves. We dam up the river of creative energy and row our boats on stagnant ponds. It's the end of growth, the end of real creativity. We've retired to well-insulated islands of success.

There's nothing wrong with success. Every human being should strive to better his or her life, but success should teach important lessons. First, it doesn't make us happy. Second, it tests our growth power. Can we still change? Are we willing to still take chances? Artists painting the same picture twenty years later have traded creativity for technical proficiency. They're no longer artists. They've become fat-cat painters afraid to experiment with success. The same can be said for doctors, lawyers, and business-men. It's easy to be satisfied with success. It's hard to take chances.

It takes courage to expand our capacity as human beings, to sustain a life full of wonder and wonderment, a life that's creative and continuously growing. It takes guts to connect our conscious-ness with infinite energy in the universe, but all else limits us to life's brief span between birth and death. Whatever we have is taken away from us, anyway, and most people are afraid of this. They shudder at the thought that "one day I'll be no more." They cling to life no matter how terrible life is for them.

Success is a momentary buffer against nothingness, but success cannot withstand the onslaught of death. No matter what tactic it takes, it still unravels at the seams. It's why happiness is the only real success. It doesn't depend on external things. It's a permanent inner state of openness, a oneness with God, and a connection to transcendental consciousness.

Work Brings More Work

There's no limit to the creative energy in a human being except the limitations the mind imprints on our consciousness. People often ask me, "How do you teach on four continents, run a busi-ness, write and publish books, and have a family?" The truth is, I never feel like I'm doing enough. There's always room to expand. Satisfaction limits life to old, boring, and repetitive activities. The only thing that grows is one's ass.

Rudi wrote at the beginning of his book, *Spiritual Cannibalism*: "Work brings more work." His words are almost sacrilegious in our modern world, a world obsessed with leisure, with four-hour work days, three-day work weeks, and one-week years, a world brainwashed into believing the less effort you make the better life is. We spend three, four, five hours a day gaping at TVs. There's nothing to do, nowhere to go, and we complain about every inconvenience, about the idea of hard work, pressure, the demands life makes. We lounge in self-imposed, non-doing states of inertia. The mind atrophies, the body disassembles, the heart grows weak, and there's nothing left of us but a tongue that refuses to stop complaining. We point fingers at everyone but ourselves.

A human being is a remarkable work of art. He has endless resources at his disposal. But he settles into a self-serving, vertiginous, humdrum mode of living. He's a somnambulist of sorts. He strolls through dreams of easy living, of non-functional shortcuts to nowhere. He pays a serious price for his laziness, a price more dear than the price of work. His entire being atrophies. He's left with nothing but memories of his former self.

People say to me, "I don't have time to meditate." They have a date, a party, the theatre, a social club, a TV show to watch, homework, and on and on. It's all bullshit. We live according to priorities. When something means enough to us, we go to any length to get it. Most people's lives are a reflection of ineptitude, a patchwork quilt of excuses for not working, not growing, and not functioning at a high level of creativity.

At the same time, it's important to know one's limitations. If our budget permits a five-hundred-dollar-a-month rent expenditure, it's senseless to look on Park Avenue for an apartment. Why waste time? We can rent an apartment for seven- or eight-hundred dollars a month. That forces us to stretch. It also lets us work within the realms of the possible. Once we're comfortable at eight-hundred dollars a month, we can move on.

My life in Denton, Texas was one of non-stop work. I developed meditation centers in Denton, Dallas, Austin, and Nacogdoches, and then set up meditation programs in prisons, halfway houses, reform schools, hospitals, and universities. I worked eighteen hours a day. My schedule included two meditation classes a day in Denton, running a business, tending to other programs, lecturing, and writing. Now, my life takes me to four continents. I also have a family, still run a business, still teach meditation every day, write, and lecture. People telephone and ask, "When are you coming to Brazil? Israel? San Francisco? Chicago? Miami? Eugene, Oregon?" I no longer live in Texas, but my work's expanded all over the globe. "Work brings more work," it has been said. It certainly does. It brings wonderful work, important work. We just have to grow strong enough to do it.

Conscious Work

Shiva has eight arms, many eyes, four heads, perfect balance, and he dances at the center of the universe. His dance is the dance of life and death. We all participate in that dance, some of us more, some of us less. It depends on our depth of consciousness and openness, the strength of our chakra systems, the quietness of mind and emotion, and our ability to stay centered and draw upon higher energy in the universe. It's not a dance for the timid, for those who hide in shadows and peek out at the world. It's a joyous celebration of opposites, the union of yin/yang, of God and His consort, of Uma/Maheshvara, of the death and rebirth of consciousness. It's a dance that celebrates wholeness of being and the human transformed into the divine.

Life provides all the puzzle pieces we need to work out our karma. They're mostly right in front of our noses. We just have to see them. The rest is conscious work, gratitude, and a joyous sense of work that leads to more work. Life's spectacle is our playground. It's not just being busy. What I mean is unconditional work, surrender through work, being grateful for work, taking joy in work, learning to use work to serve higher energy in the universe.

Most workaholics hate their jobs. They simply bury themselves in work. It's an obsessive output of nervous energy, a way of hiding from themselves, a way of burning out, of driving themselves and the people around them crazy. It's a death-in-life experience. It usually kills people long before they should die. There's no balance, harmony, or deep gratitude for work and its rewards; it's not taking simple quiet joy in work well done. Workaholics are often lonely and frightened people. They deny themselves the full length and breadth of their humanity. They forget why they took the job in the first place. Their environment's a tension-filled hub of humans that strive for goals that lead to dead ends. There's little joy, little happiness. There's only obsessive work that burns excessive tension and reduces people to caricatures of their former selves.

Conscious work is another matter entirely. It's not tension-filled striving after illusive goals. It's moment-to-moment transformation of pressure and responsibility into spiritual energy. We're forced to deepen our inner lives, to recognize the source of our energy, strengthen the chakra system, and transform mammoth responsibilities into small particles of dust.

"Make ashrams," Rudi told me when I lived in Texas. I didn't have to ask him why he wanted ashrams. I accepted the task and developed meditation teachers, then started groups in three different cities. I loved the work. It was a way to perform unconditional service, a way to contribute to life. When Rudi came to Texas, we'd fly from city to city. He'd lecture and teach with light in his eyes and joy in his heart and he, too, loved the work. I never considered the ashrams "mine." Rudi was my teacher, and I surrendered the rewards of my work to him. I learned the true nature of unconditional service on Earth.

Work is vital to life, but unconditional work is a path to God. Many people think I'm crazy. Sometimes, I wonder myself, but without service, my karma would get stuck in a rut and I'd never learn to surrender on Earth. It's important for me to have many different projects going on at the same time. One nurtures the other.

My teaching nurtures my writing, my writing nurtures my business, and my family nurtures my friendships. If I'm bogged down in one project, I turn to another. There's always fresh energy, rejuvenation, and a newness about things. Great artists often work on many canvases at once. One inspires the other. When inspiration lags, they turn to another project. It injects fresh energy into their blood. Projects, like human beings, need time to mature. If we force them too much, inspiration and creativity begin to strain. They resemble a beaten, dead horse.

We're born on the Earth to learn to serve. Wittingly or unwittingly, we serve some part of life, but unconditional service teaches unconditional love. It expects nothing in return for time spent helping other people, and it lifts the consciousness of a human being bogged down in self-interest. It teaches humility and gratitude. There's real power in humility, power so strong it could change the most headstrong of people, power derived from gratitude and from the consciousness of God at the source of all things.

I once said to Rudi, "With power like this, you could easily become a dictator." "What a bore!" he answered. "What a waste of life and karma!'"

If "God is love," and the spectacle of God is all around us, then everything is steeped in love. Our work is to bow to God's love in the hearts of men. It's to forgive and have patience and not judge the mistakes of others, to be free of ourselves and be one with God, to be a vehicle for spiritual energy, and never, not for a moment, think we are doing it. It's to trust the world and its lessons; to surrender opinion and ego; and to be grateful for every breath, every morsel of food, and every experience (both positive and negative); and recognize it as our teacher.

I always understood this, but to live it was another matter. It took years of meditation practice to recognize that to serve higher energy is more important than my own need for power. I am nothing but a speck in a timeless universe. I've been let down by hundreds of people in my life, yet meditation practice has given me the strength to survive impossible situations, a strength derived from strong chakras, from years of inner work, from a one-pointed need to be with God.

I often ask myself, "What do you want to serve in life? Do you want to serve people, ego, power, money, or energy of a higher nature?" The answer's simple. I serve what has yet to abandon me, what's always there, what guides me through every crisis, what forces me to grow and to change my life, what makes me feel love in my heart and be happy to be alive.

Just What You Need

I'd been in Texas for about six months. It was Christmas time and the entire meditation group had planned to take a trip to New York to see Rudi. We would drive cross-country and I needed forty dollars as my share of the expenses. I didn't have a penny. At seven A.M., about an hour before we were going to leave on the trip, a woman walked briskly up to my house. "I know you're leaving today," she said, "but I couldn't sleep last night. I have to have this table." (I operated an antique-and-used-furniture shop from my house.) She pointed to a little bedside commode that cost exactly forty dollars. She pulled out the money, gave it to me, took the table, and disappeared into the great yawn of Denton, Texas. I thought I was in a dream. I quickly gave the forty dollars to the guy who drove the car. "Let's go to New York!" I said. "Let's go see Rudi!"

Spiritual work gives you just what you need. Rarely, if ever, does it make gluttons out of people. It makes sure you have enough to continue the voyage. It keeps you slightly hungry. It keeps you from becoming a fat cat.

I've had millions of dollars come through my hands in my lifetime. It's always had one purpose: to support my teaching, to provide meditation classes for serious students and myself. I could easily have bought Rolls Royces, fine antiques, or a beautiful house in the suburbs, but I've never felt a need for that kind of security. My inner work is all the security I need. The meditation classes are important for my spiritual development. They also have forced me to learn how to make money.

As a young man, the idea of business repulsed me, but I found myself in Denton with a large meditation center on my hands. Rent had to be paid, food bought, utilities and taxes paid. I developed businesses to support the situation. I learned how to make money. Now, years later, my expenses have increased considerably, but money still has one function in my life: to make sure there's a place for spiritual work. This doesn't negate family, cars, wonderful places to live and work, antiques, and other signs of success, but the prime purpose of money is to give life. It is not a goal unto itself. It's just a tool that makes meditation classes possible.

A human being must learn to bear full responsibility for himself and his loved ones. That's part of the spiritual process. If he trusts higher energy, it'll take care to provide. It has for me. But there's no way to escape hard work. Laziness is not conducive to inner development. Nor does it provide money and success. It's important to learn to work consciously; it's important to understand the real reasons to make money.

Stuart Perrin

CHAPTER SEVEN:

The Goals of Spiritual Work

The first goal in the development of higher consciousness is freeing ourselves of neurotic and anxiety-ridden inner lives. As stated previously, we are the problem, but we are also the solution to the problem. If we get to the other side of ourselves, there's a clear-running field to enlightenment.

The mind's never-ending chitchat eats away at well-being. It often creates tensions which test the scope of human endurance. We run from them. We hide in well-insulated corridors created from fear, but there's nothing wrong with emotional, physical, and mental problems. No one on Earth can escape them. They should inspire us to work on ourselves. Most people in meditation class are here because they have problems. Without them, we'd live like cabbages, like heads of lettuce, like barnyard animals that graze, sleep, and while away the day. Problems are the first barrier to higher consciousness. As we master them, we move on to spiritual realms; we free ourselves from ourselves as we travel the path to enlightenment.

Though people need a steady diet of meditation to quell the mind's chatterbox, it's difficult to get them to work consistently on themselves. Without it, the mind enslaves them in vicious cycles of self-induced egomania. There's no escaping corridors lined with masks that depict our neurotic states of being.

Students of meditation often miss the point of inner work. Though they're physically present in meditation class, their minds drift all over the map. They're in a fight with someone, they daydream and project financial wellbeing, or worry about business deals and relationships. They're not focused on the navel chakra. Then they wonder why the meditation practice doesn't work. Most of their questions reflect a lack of focus.

Meditation is not a passive experience. It's work and more work to open areas within us that have been closed most of our lives. In time, we get older, thicker, less supple, more conservative, and protective of ourselves, and the chakra system atrophies. The mind's subtle, almost devious, activity steals love and joy from us. It turns us into sterile replicas of our former selves. We're faced with an uphill battle. We have to resurrect the child in us, the life-affirming, innocent babe that's not afraid to experiment with the world, the child who's been buried beneath layers of neurotic tension.

Every meditation practitioner needs a master to guide him or her on the path, someone to correct bad habits, and someone who's been over the path himself, who continues to grow every day, to surrender and to devote his energy to serving God. The mind's devious nature keeps us from seeing clear light. We latch on to illusion and convince ourselves it's real. We forget easily. We're swept away by intense emotion, by mental hubris dressed to please. A teacher reminds us of our spiritual path. His presence forces us to get our lives together.

One Taste of God

My problems are secondary to my goal of spiritual enlighten- ment. Though they're more immediate, they're still not the reason I practice meditation. Rudi once said to me, "One taste of God, just one taste, makes everything else silly."

The question is, how does one get a taste of God?

It takes seven years of schooling to become a lawyer and twelve years to get a degree in medicine. Then the work really begins. A plumber is dangerous if he hasn't mastered his craft, as is a sur- geon, architect, engineer, waiter, or glazier. These professions are easier to master than a spiritual life. The quest for God is the most difficult quest of all. We have to get training in the fine art of inner work. We have to master the mind and breath, open the chakra system, get past our tension, and learn to serve in the world.

People ask, "Why do I need to study with a guru?" The answer's simple. Human beings are the single most difficult creatures on Earth. When they look inside themselves, they see confusion. When they look outside themselves, they see more confusion. It's easy to judge others, but almost impossible to unravel our own inner lives. That's why we need teachers. They show us the path. They help us get past ourselves. They guide us to the precincts of higher consciousness and God. It's a lifetime's work. It takes a very serious commitment. It's not like tennis lessons or racquetball lessons, or being a student of *mahjong*, or learning to bake bread. No one will learn to master Kundalini meditation in an adult education class at New York University.

People often ask, "How much does it cost to study in your classes?" "Not much," I tell them, "about a dollar to a dollar-and-a-half per class. But there are other costs, hidden ones, intangible costs, based on surrender and gratitude. If you want a spiritual life, eventually it's got to cost you everything."

If a guru declared he could enlighten a disciple for a mere million dollars, if he could deliver the goods, a million dollars is a dirt-cheap price to pay for the greatest treasure on Earth. Job surrendered everything but his faith in God; Jesus gave his life. There's no easy way. Nothingness means total surrender, it means we have to let go of all attachments to the Earth. No ordinary person can pay so steep a price. It takes exceptional courage. Even a saint has to surrender his saintliness; a holy man, his holiness; a beggar, his begging bowl; a rich man, his castle; the Pope, his Popedom; a wise man, his wisdom; a powerful man, his power.

People pay a high price for fame and fortune. They'll do most anything for it. They'll cheat, steal, kill, and swindle, whatever the Machiavellian dictate demands. Whatever tools necessity provides, they'll use them to step over other people, to ridicule them, to beat them when they're down, and to march victoriously to the top of the heap. Then they become fair game for ambitious Lilliputians that struggle to the top of the same mountain.

Most people are not ready to tackle a spiritual life. They've yet to find the need within themselves. It's a question of evolution of consciousness. When a person's ready, nothing stops them from traveling the spiritual path. Sometimes it takes hundreds, if not thousands of lifetimes for us to get ready. Each lifetime is another department in the university called Earth, another opportunity to develop consciousness, another opportunity to free ourselves from karmic rounds of suffering and pain.

As a young man, I used to think, "There's nowhere to hide, nowhere to run, nothing but earth beneath my feet and sky above my head. I'm a little boy lost in a muddle of my own making. I can't hide in the suburbs or in a village or hamlet far from the city. There's always me, ever-present me, that stares at me wherever I go. When I'm ready, I'll hear the voice of God. Up until then, I don't know what. I'll listen, that's all; I'll listen and learn and do whatever I can to get ready."

I once believed people were ignorant of spiritual practice. I believed they could be awakened, but I've come to find out that's not the case. I've discovered most people are not ready for deep inner meditation practice. I've discovered spiritual work is a byproduct of evolution. I've discovered nothing on Earth stops a person who's tasted the nectar of God; nothing interferes with his commitment to a spiritual life.

Responsibility to God is a terrifying thought, one that would disrupt the bowels of a character in a Dostoyevsky novel. Imagine not being able to turn your back on God. Imagine a life of total honesty, truthfulness, trust, and forgiveness. A life like that is beyond our comprehension. At best, it is a laundry list of words that sound good, words so strong they could traumatize the entire human race.

I've heard people say, "I live in the guru's grace; therefore, I'll get enlightened." But people often use the guru as an excuse to avoid their own inner work. Rudi once told me, "When you sunbathe in the light of the guru's grace, the only thing that grows is your ass.'"

Life is the guru's grace, life in all its abundance, but life demands that we work on ourselves. Life reminds us how little we know, how much we have to learn, how subtle are the ways of God on Earth, how vast the horizon in front of us.

A commitment to spiritual practice takes years of evolution. We make left turns and right turns. We sail on estuaries that lead to a plethora of dead ends. We try every department in the University of Earth, until all that's left is infinite energy in the universe, until we finally travel the allegorical crossroads to a place in the heart connected to God. We exhaust illusion's promise and want a glimpse of truth, something real, something that doesn't lead to dead ends. Deep meditation practice still frightens novices. They're familiar with death's dark passage, with despair, loneliness, pain, anxiety, and countless other syncopated dance steps that take them nowhere. Meditation practice demands honesty, truth, and reversal of death's dark ways. We've got to emerge from the shadow side of life into light and joy. We've got to love ourselves and other people. The idea frightens most human beings. How do they trust? How can they be honest with themselves after years of self-deception? It's difficult to change inside. One has to dredge up old demons and wash them out to sea. One has to learn to be a happy person.

Most people say, "Yeah. I want that," but when they discover the work involved in serious meditation practice, they look for something easier, less demanding, some form of meditation that'll insulate their persona.

Superficial answers satisfy less committed seekers. They live on a spiritual diet equivalent to water and potatoes. They eat and eat and starve to death as they chew and swallow their food. Evolution's an intangible force that controls all our lives, a force that determines who's ready to practice deep spiritual work, and who isn't.

Stuart Perrin

CHAPTER EIGHT:

A Human Being Living a Happy Life

Joy is the language of God on Earth, joy and unconditional love at the center of the human heart. It is a language rarely spoken by people, but, a language we have to learn if we're going to be spiritually enlightened, a language that must be spoken by human beings to other human beings, a language that communicates the essence of things.

The slow evolution of consciousness from depression to joy, from neurosis to inner peace and quiet, from the mind's existential outhouse to the heart's warmth is all about openness and acceptance of life and all its responsibilities. A human being feels compassion for his fellow man. He never judges nor does he suffer from megalomaniacal visions of himself and his position on Earth. He listens to God's voice all the time, rejoices in it, and responds with words from the center of his heart. You can't pretend to be human. You can't substitute the heart's precious emission of love with false vocal tones. People know the difference. Muzak-like love vows usually fall on deaf ears. You can't play-act humility, gratitude, joy, and happiness. They've a ring of truth about them. They're like a bell that echoes in a country sky, a bell that speaks directly to the human heart.

These are ideal traits. No one can live up to them, not in a world in which the ideal exists outside human comprehension. But they are goals. As we get closer to them, we get closer to our own humanity.

The heart won't stay open without strong inner foundation and balance, without *chi* that emits from the *hara*. Rudi always compared it to a flower. "There are roots, a stem, leaves, and flowers," he said. "Without roots, flowers are impossible."

External events do not infringe on real happiness. A happy person can be alone or in a crowd of thousands of people. It's all the same to him. Neither steals the joy in his heart. The wind is his friend, the sky, the earth, the sound of *Om* from the source of creation, cars zoom past, trees that rustle, grass that blows, city noise, country sounds, village and town hubbub. He never feels alone. A happy person witnesses the spectacle of God's creation. He's never separate from it. Saint Francis spoke to birds. Christ spoke to the human heart. Everything was a joy to them because they were alive, happy, and part of God's creation. They were fully-evolved human beings.

Meditation and yoga work together to open the heart chakra. When the human heart's closed, a certain deadness pervades. Joy disappears. Love cringes in a corner. Lacking emotional ease, it dares not come out.

There are thousands of arcane books written on the mysteries of the cosmos, on philosophical and theological isms, but intellectual understanding bypasses one simple reality: the day we learn to be happy is the day we've learned everything we have to learn on Earth. Our karma is finished. We've graduated from the University of Samsara.

The human mind can't grasp love. It can analyze it, dissect it, wring it out, and stuff it into an intellectual meat grinder, but to sustain heartfelt joy every day is perhaps the most difficult thing to do on Earth. It's a noble undertaking––a quiet, but profound wisdom few people grasp and even fewer live with on a day-to-day basis.

The Sweet Center

We can escape from everything in life but ourselves. No matter where we go, we're the one piece of baggage we can't leave behind. Though customs, language, costumes, borders, topography, and terrain all change, the one thing that doesn't change is our inner lives. If we can't sustain joy, love, and gratitude, no change of environment is going to make things better. After the initial thrill, we still have to look at ourselves in the mirror. If we're not happy, the mirror reflects the dark inner world of unhappiness. It's us staring at us. No job, no environment, and no amount of money will change our inner lives. They'll turn us on for a few moments. Then we've got to return to a reality that speaks in a harsh voice, a reality we can't escape from no matter where we run. Are we happy? Is the chakra system open? Have we built within ourselves a strong spiritual life? These are questions that never go away. We try to avoid them, but they always remind us of how full of shit we are.

The mind's a powerful tool if used to develop an inner life, but the mind's also a Pandora's box of conflicting messages. It has all and none of the answers at the same time. Its voice never shuts up. Though we stuff ourselves with uppers and downers, with antidepressants and amphetamines, though we drink, smoke cigarettes and marijuana, nothing stops the mind's terrible voice. It's like a science-fiction movie that stars a cast of characters Hollywood could never invent. We are center stage. We're surrounded by demons too numerous to take on in battle.

The mind identifies with negativity because negativity's on the surface of life. It doesn't take a genius to pick out life's abundant peccadilloes. But the mind's energy can open the chakra system. When used as an instrument of meditation, the mind becomes an extraordinary life-giving force, a surgical instrument capable of cutting through blocks of inner tension. It can free us from ourselves, and what's killing us begins to give us life.

God waits patiently for each human soul to evolve. Just as a pear has to ripen on a tree before we pick and eat it, we also have to mature and ripen. Premature picking makes for sour pears and bitter people. Rudi once said, "It takes nine months to have a baby and one second to die."

God welcomes our soul just as we welcome harvests of fruit and vegetables. In every generation, a few human beings have spiritual lives. The rest of mankind evolves from lifetime to lifetime. It slowly, gradually, finds a path into the precincts of the divine, but first it needs to become human.

The dictionary tags us all as human beings, but tags, rarely, if ever, tell the truth about products. We adopt personas, and wear costumes woven from threads of ego, and masks that hide layers of tension. False images of self are presented to a world that worships persona, that deifies ego, that wallows in illusion, and believes illusion's stink to be reality. We bitch and complain about everything that life gives us. No matter how much money we make, no matter how comfortable we are, there's always something else to complain about. We lack spiritual training. We assume what we're born with is what we'll always be. We assume a human being is the sum of his or her gifts, but that's foolhardy. We all have minds, breath, and chakras, but few of us have training. Few of us know what to do with our minds and breath and chakras. We never look beyond the stink pile of mental and material illusion.

It's easy to immerse ourselves in the material world, but we forget that matter rots. We forget that most ancient civilizations are in ruins. We forget life's short seventy-year span is like a drop of water in an ocean. We forget the material world's a tiny part of overall consciousness, a gift given to those with spiritual ambition, a prison to those who transform God into matter.

The material world's nothing more than physical form imbued with spirit. When the spirit departs, the material world, no matter how vast and opulent, crumbles at the feet of men.

Buried beneath tension's rubble is a rich, profound, incredibly beautiful, energy-filled cauldron of truth and wisdom. We're like watermelons, coconuts, pecans, and pistachios. We have to be broken open to get to the meat or juice. Did you ever eat an artichoke? Its heart is at the center of layer upon layer of bitter peels. The closer we get to the center, the sweeter and more delicious the artichoke becomes. The heart is a delicacy, a treat worth waiting for. We're very much like artichokes. We're thick-skinned, boorish, opinionated beasts full of sarcasm, skepticism, cynicism, and distrust—all right on the surface—a mask we wear to protect ourselves from being hurt. We think we're smarter and better than everyone else, but it's all armor that rusts in the weather, armor that comes apart at the seams, and leaves us naked in an indifferent world.

Beneath the armor is a child full of love, a child that sings the song of life's inimitable pleasure dome, a child who loves to dance, to play, to enjoy life's simple splendors, a child that lives in the center of our hearts, a child full of love, joy and boundless happiness, a child buried beneath thick skin, ego, cynicism, and distrust. If we fail to embrace that child, we never recognize the wonders of God on Earth.

What is it we really want out of life? All desires, every goal, the people and things we cherish, are supposed to make us happy. They rarely, if ever, do. We alone can make ourselves happy. Once we learn this, we can share joy and happiness with other human beings. We stop searching for the elusive butterfly. We've discovered happiness exists within ourselves.

Plato, Aristotle, Spinoza, and most every other philosopher and literary genius concluded happiness is the ultimate goal of humanity. I was nineteen years old when I first read this. I became irate. I said to myself, "I don't believe it! There has to be something else!" Now, after many years of working on myself, I've arrived at the same conclusion: an enlightened person is a person that leads a happy life.

A happy person's finished the course at Earth University. He has nothing to come back for. He has learned to speak the language of God. He's free of his karma and he can embrace the infinite.

When we love another person, we forgive them the most glaring of faults. The heart doesn't see negative energy. It loves, that's all, and that love is nonjudgmental.

When the heart closes, we often detest the traits we once loved in another person. What once turned us on now drives us crazy. A person's smell, a birthmark, the sound of their voice, the cutesy little behavioral patterns we once adored—all of it's transformed into a minor-league horror show. There's no explaining why we detest the things we once loved. Instead of joy and love, instead of acceptance and patience, we're reduced to petty tyrants that hone in on the faults of others. Instead of being grateful to God for breath, food, touch, taste, smell, sight, and hearing, for the clothing on our backs, our health, for the place we live, we complain all the time. We become overbearing, petty, and absurd little creatures that somehow flourish in self-induced hell.

Happy people are not idiot savants, simpletons, or lobotomized potatoheads that stare into space twenty-four hours a day. They work, they struggle, and they take on responsibility, but they perform these impossible feats with an open heart.

What Two Drunken Fools Knew

There are two legendary monks in the Japanese Zen Buddhist tradition. I can never remember their names, but they're always painted like drunken fools with brooms in their hands, two blissed out, happy monks who swept the monastery floor as if God Himself ran the place.

When the head abbot died, a convergence of high-ranking monks met to choose another abbot. They weighed all possibilities and came up empty. No high-ranking monk in the monastery personified the Zen ethic. They all understood Zen but did not live its principles. After weeks of deliberating, after consulting with astrologers, psychics, and important monks all over the country, they could not find a successor to the dead abbot.

The two monks continued to sweep and clean. Wide-eyed and drunk on God's energy, they felt joy and love for every person and creature in the monastery. They were both happy. Sweeping the floor was a sacred act. Their beings resonated with Zen. They lived in the moment. The other monks thought about Zen. They had hundreds of answers to questions asked. They were wise, erudite, profound, and full of Zen-like theories on life and death, but the two drunken fools had no answers. They knew nothing; they denied having wisdom of any sort. The two monks swept the floor like the floor was made of gold.

The other monks began to take notice. After a while, the ranking monks realized the two drunken fools lived in the light of Zen. They were the only monks in the monastery drunk on God's energy. The ranking monks chose the drunken fools to head the monastery. They made the right choice! The two fools became legend. They ran the monastery in the light of Zen.

Most of us interpret God; we don't experience God. But spiritual work is about learning to experience higher energy on Earth; it's about becoming a happy person.

This has nothing to do with IQ or physical beauty. It has to do with an open heart, with a sparkle in the eye, with drunken wisdom, with the divine light of higher creative energy that emanates from the core of one's being. I've never seen an open-hearted person who is not physically beautiful. There's a child-like glow, innocence, love, and richness of spirit coming through them.

Happy people are like the drunken fools that once swept the floor of the monastery, kind and beloved fools, who, in their own way, are reminders of God's energy manifesting on Earth. Most people short-circuit happiness. They don't believe they're worthy of it. They're afraid other people will take advantage of them if they're open. Ironically, people can only take advantage of us when we're closed. They can leech on to our tension, manipulate our insecurities, and play mental and psychic games with our inferiorities. An open person has nothing for them to grab on to. An open person is detached from emotional and mental problems. They're in a state of surrender, free of themselves and of the world. No one can take away from us possessions we're not attached to; no one can hurt us if we're not fearful. We can only be hurt if we're protective of ourselves, if we hide in the womb of our own anxiety, if we set up psychological barriers between ourselves and life.

Spiritual maturity disengages us from the world's nonsense. It simplifies daily living. We do our jobs and love our families. We are nonjudgmental, conscious, and grateful for small and large things. We try not to live in a rut; we try to tap the deepest resource of creative energy available to us in the moment. There'll always be something wrong in life. That's part of the test of living. Perfection is either a state of mind or a sky full of angels. It has nothing to do with living on Earth. In Macbeth, Shakespeare wrote: "Life's but a walking shadow, a poor player that struts and frets his hour upon the stage and then is heard no more. It is a tale told by an idiot, full of sound and fury, signifying nothing." Nobody's ever put it more succinctly. But if we open our hearts, at least we can enjoy this idiotic tale, at least we can enjoy the "sound and fury," the spectacle, the "walking shadow" called life!

People often ask me, "How do you achieve this? How do you become a happy person?" It's a good question. But there's no easy answer. It's not like turning a light switch on and off.

The Merry-Go-Round of Pain

Most people talk ad infinitum about their problems but do little or nothing to resolve them. They're at loss to make sense of an absurd world. Tension builds up to unsupportable levels. People get migraines, ulcers, heart conditions, Alzheimer's, strokes, and numerous other illnesses brought on by out-of-control anxiety. Suffering is pandemic and it touches people who wallow in complicated labyrinths that go nowhere. They've forgotten how to listen to anything but the confusion in their own minds. Then they dump bushel loads of futility into the ears of weary listeners. Lack of consciousness plagues the entire human race, a plague doctors have no arsenal to combat. They've tried therapy, drugs, and institutions; they've tried everything but teaching people to open their hearts. The confusion seems to get worse. There's more anxiety, neurosis, and insecurity than ever. People have grown more isolated from each other. Money injected into the healing arts has one purpose: to make more money—to create a business so vast and powerful it controls the mindset of the human race. To tell people that drugs, surgery, and institutionalized care will make them better is to tell them anything but the truth, the truth being, "Open your heart, be grateful, fill yourself with love and joy, and most of your problems will go away."

The human race spends billions of dollars to cure itself of mental, emotional, and sexual disorders. But billions of dollars won't buy happiness; billions of dollars can't buy an open heart. Billions of dollars buys pills, rest cures, surgery, doctors' time, and mega hospital equipment. It doesn't help us love our family. It doesn't help us master our problems. It doesn't stop the flood of verbal tension that pours from our mouths, tension that not only makes our life unbearable, but the lives, as well, of everyone around us.

It's impossible to love others if most of our time is spent beating one's self up. If there's no self-worth, the consciousness of a human being lingers in hellish arenas fabricated by the mind. We forget to breathe, we forget to listen, and we forget to open our hearts and be grateful. We forget breath is prayer. We forget that every human being, religious and non-religious alike, is praying twenty-four hours a day. We forget that our breath sustains life, that our breath is the rhythm of the universe.

Gratitude gets lost in the business of daily living. We too often take the people we love and ourselves for granted. Their uniqueness disappears in a blurred setting, and we no longer are conscious of individual effort. Our hearts close, and all we see are faults.

It's easy to forget the uniqueness in people we love. They're close to us and often threaten us and force us to give from places within ourselves we're afraid to enter. They demand love from us, and love is difficult to sustain. Love is a force more powerful than any other force on Earth. We have to be spiritually strong to love other human beings. We have to awaken a higher power within us. We have to love ourselves first, and then we can love family and friends. There's no one we can blame for our own unhappiness. We were born with all necessary tools to work on ourselves. The great mystery is why people don't use these tools to open their hearts. Proper use of mind and breath, gratitude and a strong chakra system will develop their humanity. But almost no one does it. Here lies one of the great mysteries on Earth: given the gift of life, we use that gift to make others and ourselves miserable. We rarely, if ever, use that gift to grow spiritually.

The dynamics of freedom have been lost in a religious, economic, and racial blur. We're always trying to get free of external things and rarely talk about getting free of ourselves. Racial and economic freedoms do little to resolve inner conflict. They don't clear up the psychological mess that clutters the minds of people. In fact, there will never be racial or economic freedom until people learn to be happy within themselves, until people stop being prisoners of their own righteousness.

We live in a quick-fix society in which hard work and commitment are pariahs. The idea of spiritual work is an oxymoron. There's little or no comprehension of its meaning. People's attitude is often: If you pay me fifteen dollars an hour to have a spiritual life, I'll work at it. If you pay me a hundred dollars an hour, I'll work even harder." If the teacher says, "You're going to learn to open your heart and be happy. That's the greatest treasure life has to offer," people answer, "I want a car, a TV, a set of golf clubs, a lifetime pass to Knicks and Yankees games, opera tickets, theatre tickets, sushi…that will make me happy! Spiritual work? What the hell is spiritual work?"

People grow old coveting illusion. They shit out sushi and exhaust themselves screaming at Knicks games, and never, not for a second, do people think, "I can eat divine sushi and also do deep spiritual work." One doesn't negate the other. Then age sets in, the chakra system deteriorates, and we no longer have energy to work on ourselves.

Each moment of life is precious. How we use the moment determines whether or not we become spiritually enlightened.

A happy person is a successful person, a person who's found God inside and outside of himself and has no regrets leaving the world. The final goal of evolution on Earth is happiness. Once it's attained, we graduate to higher realms of consciousness. Once it's attained, there's no reason for us to return to life's merry-go-round of pain and suffering.

An Exercise to Become More Human

Kundalini yoga is a technique that unifies diverse aspects of ourselves by conscious use of energy. It's a practical work that uses mind and breath to open the chakras. It eliminates right and wrong, both of which are creations of the mind, both of which are limited to the mind's understanding of life, both of which create barriers of fear, and both of which create self-righteousness. It fosters dialectic; it unifies polarities; and it creates oneness instead of diverse and conflicted ideas that keep people at war with one another. Kundalini yoga creates an all-inclusive world in which pieces of life's puzzle fit together in relative harmony. There's no right and no wrong, just life in all its dimensions and peculiarities. Things are what they are. Even conflict is part of the design. The moment we judge, our view of life gets complicated. Our judgments fog up reality with self-induced ideas and opinions that mean nothing to other people.

Kundalini yoga teaches harmony and balance. If we create our own reality, and if we project that reality into life, then we can change that reality by transforming tension into spirit. Kundalini yoga is a technique of inner work, a meditation practice that develops *chi*. It builds harmony and balance within a human being and teaches us to use breath and mind to connect with transcendental energy in the universe.

Throughout history, men and women have used horrendous circumstances as springboards to sainthood. In the movie *Schindler's List*, a petty German hustler of a businessman in World War II becomes human when he realizes his Jewish employees are also human. Their lives are more important than money-making scams. By the movie's end, he's obsessed with helping Jews escape Nazi persecution. His greed disappears in compassion for the plight of persecuted peoples. Horrendous circumstances forced him to find his own humanity. In contrast, a Nazi officer took pot-shots at Jews from his balcony. He considered them to be less than human, as animals, insects, a scourge let loose on the human race. Reality depends on individual viewpoints. Schindler used the horror of Nazi persecution as an excuse to become more human. The Nazi officer took delight in killing Jews. Both were right in their own minds, but Schindler learned compassion. His human-ity came to the fore. It gave him nobility of soul.

There's no one way to view the world. What's right and wrong, what's positive and negative, are simply states of mind. But the heart doesn't judge. The heart teaches us to be more human. Schindler's compassion arose from looking evil directly in the eye and not being afraid. Without Nazi fanaticism staring him in the face, his nobility of soul may never have surfaced. Fascist horrors turned him into a saintly person. The question always is this: How does one behave if there's no sense of right and wrong? But this question is posed by the human mind. The heart would never ask questions like that. It would never dwell on good and evil. The heart can't even conceive of them. Given half a chance, the human heart would forgive every fanatical son-of-a-bitch responsible for suffering on Earth. Only the mind seeks revenge, a mind that preaches "an eye for an eye," a mind incapable of forgiving, incapable of loving one's enemy.

Opinions are formulated by mind. They change as our view of reality changes. But the human heart has no opinions. It's full of love, joy, forgiveness, and compassion, and it refuses to dwell on wrongdoing. When the heart's open, the Earth itself becomes paradise. Conflict vanishes, and opinion becomes nonsensical expression voiced by unhappy people afraid to go deep enough within themselves to be grateful for their lives.

Meditation in Prison

Years ago, I learned an important lesson: if anything positive happens to me, it'll be followed by a negative experience. One attracts the other. I've learned to live without expectations, to take life as it comes, to free myself of opinion, to break down preconception, and to live my life moment to moment. It took a great weight off my shoulders. I can now act quietly and consciously. I can approach situations with love and understanding. I've learned to trash preconceived notions of what's right or wrong.

Though society fosters competition as a healthy economic vehicle, the pressures of competition deteriorate mental and physical well-being. They take their toll. The body breaks down. The mind lapses into black holes of forgetfulness. There's jealousy, backbiting, ass-kissing, and hundreds of other reactions to competitive society. People are nervous wrecks. They can't handle the pressure. But in truth, no one is in competition with anyone else. There's abundance enough to provide for every living person. If we get past ourselves, the rest is easy. We can succeed in life without shredding our minds and bodies. The first step is internal, to build a strong inner life. The object is to get balanced, open the heart chakra, quiet the mind, listen to the voice of silence that emerges from transcendental planes of consciousness, and create a bridge from meditation practice to every other area of life. Rudi once said, "It's a miracle anyone survives a day."

The internal war rages without rhyme or reason; it continues day and night to strip us of physical and mental well-being. What we see is what we are, but it's hard to take a good look. People are frightened of themselves. They want to be pampered and cuddled and told the pain will pass, but pain lingers until the day we die. We have to make friends with it; we have to detach ourselves from its gnawing presence.

Years ago, I taught meditation in a Texas prison to bank robbers, Mafia goons, cocaine peddlers, prostitutes, ex-junkies, and assorted other characters from a Mickey Spillane novel. I think I learned more from those people than they learned from me. At the end of each class, twenty muscle-bound men and women lined up to hug me and say thanks. The meditation touched a very human place inside them. No one judged them. Everyone was treated equally. The students in the prison got deeply in touch with their own humanity.

Every Sunday, I'd bring a dozen or so inmates to my meditation center in Denton. I'd pick them up, drive them to Denton, and assume complete responsibility for the group. One inmate kept smoking dope. Every time I caught him, I asked him to stop. "You'll destroy this program for yourself and everyone else," I told him. He refused to stop. He just laughed and said nothing would happen.

One day, in the prison hallway, outside the chapel where I held meditation class, I met the dope-smoking inmate.

"I don't want you in class anymore," I said to him.

"What do you mean?" he asked.

"Every time you come out to my house, I find you with a joint in your mouth. I don't want it. You're going to destroy the program for everybody that's here. This program's really helping people. Why kill a good thing?" I explained.

"You don't have the guts to say this in front of everybody else," he said to me.

I replied, "Just spare yourself the embarrassment. Go away and forget about it."

"You don't have the guts," he said again.

"Okay, come on," I said.

We walked into the chapel. There were twenty inmates sitting there. "You're never to come to this meditation class again," I said to him in front of everybody. "I have tremendous respect for every person in this room. It takes guts to do what we do here. Why the hell should you destroy the program? Why the hell are you smoking dope in my house?" The guy turned white. He walked out of the room like a sheep.

Late afternoon, about three years later, I heard a knock at the door of my Denton apartment. I opened it and saw the dope-smoking inmate and a woman in the entrance.

"Hi, how ya doin'?" he said.

I said hello and shook his hand.

"Stuart," he said, "first of all, I want to introduce you to my wife. I've been telling her for three years about you. Secondly, I've come to apologize."

It just broke my heart. I almost started to cry.

"What you did in that prison was the best thing that ever happened to me in my life," he went on. "I blew it. I had to tell you I'm sorry. I apologize."

I was very moved by the courage of the man. "Come in," I said.

He and his wife sat down for tea. We talked for over an hour. He told me about his life in prison and on the streets. Before he left, he hugged me and thanked me once more.

I never saw the man again. Meditation practice had touched something deep in him. He had learned what he was supposed to learn: a little gratitude, humility, respect, and the courage to admit he was wrong. These are important lessons. Most people never learn them. Most people take gifts for granted. If nothing else, he learned no one has the right to treat cheaply the thing that's given him life.

Spiritual work is a great treasure. It must be respected, cherished, used consciously, and never taken for granted. If people want to smoke dope, that's their choice. It's not for me to judge them. At the same time, why destroy a situation that benefits many people? It's an immature expression of ego to say, "I can do what I want to do, no matter who I hurt, no matter what I destroy."

It's difficult to learn to say "no" to people close to us, but family members and friends take us for granted. They're often insensitive and full of themselves, and they trespass on our feelings. Sometimes a good "no" reminds them to stop, a "no" spoken without malice, a simple reminder to respect our space, a reminder there are limits to egotistical behavior. We don't shut the door on loved ones; we make sure they don't use us badly.

Help Me, I'm Tense

The search for truth is a quixotic voyage taken by warriors who wish to do battle with themselves. It's a romantic jousting with phantoms in fairy tales, with dragons and evil knights, with windmills and white whales. Truth eludes us no matter where we look, no matter how hard we try to find it. Without it, we stagnate. With it, we go mad and try to capture the essential nature of an ideal state that exists outside the realms of polarity. We have to learn the fine art of surrender. Ordinary logic takes us to the edge, never across. It drives us to the brink of madness. It takes us to the proverbial Kafkaesque door, but we never gain entrance. It sets up absurd borders in an absurd world in which truth languishes on the other side of reason. There's no going back and there's no going forward. We stand at the edge of a cliff, waiting for Godot. We try to figure out what to do next, but that only makes things worse; that only makes us more insane. Reasonable answers become invalid as life forces us to reconsider reality. We often cling to what was, to what doesn't work anymore, unaware that reality is now different and we must make a conscious effort to change.

Years ago, Rudi bought a small hotel in Big Indian, New York, a town located in the Catskill Mountains. He ran a meditation center there. I asked him if I could spend a week at the Big Indian Ashram. I needed to get out of New York City. I felt exhausted. The winter had been very hard for me, with work, school, and many other things. "That's what it's for," he said. "Go whenever you want to."

I took a bus to Big Indian, then walked up the hill to the ashram. After I found a room and unpacked my bag, I decided to do something constructive. A tractor sat idle in the front yard. The grass, at least an acre of it, stood three feet high. It needed cutting. It's the perfect project, I thought.

I got on the tractor, started it up, drove it through the yard, cut grass, and was very happy. About fifteen minutes into my grass cutting project, I suddenly heard a voice screaming at me. It was the ashram manager. He ran across the front yard. I stopped the tractor, got off, and waited for him. "What's the matter?" I asked. He listed about fifty things I had done wrong. "But I've only been here a half-hour," I thought. "It's impossible to have created so much havoc." He continued to scream at me; his eyes, face, and voice were full of anger. "There are one or two options," I thought. (I hadn't said a word to him yet.) "Either slug it out with this madman or keep your mouth shut and see where all this leads."

I decided to keep my mouth shut, to listen to him, to let him vent his anger. For ten minutes he blamed me for everything from Armageddon to the demise of the Western world, to the plague and bad plumbing. He exhausted all his tension and tears came into his eyes. He stopped screaming, looked at me for a moment, put his arms around my neck, hugged me, and said, "Thank you." Then he walked away.

Not only did I avoid a fistfight, I also made a friend. His anger covered up a deeper need. He was saying, "Help me, I'm tense. Are

123

you big enough to listen to me without fighting? I need someone to love me unconditionally." It was the first time in my life I kept my mouth shut, and, God knows, it worked. I ended up becoming very good friends with the guy.

CHAPTER NINE:

Being Nobody...
Knowing Nothing

Life's mystery is hidden in the unknown quantity. What we know we can fit into a teacup. The rest? Therein lies the mystery of the unknown; therein lies almost all of creative energy. The wise admit they know little or nothing about life. Fools have answers to every question. They drown in their own wisdom; they're full of themselves and they use personality and ego to lure people into their giant spider web arena. Once there, wingless flies are fed empty wisdom. The glitter of empty wisdom attracts lesser egos like lights attract moths; the glitter drains the vital juices of crippled souls. It flourishes because lesser egos sacrifice themselves to greater egos. They're too frightened to change. They're trapped in a spider web of false wisdom. A real teacher has no wisdom. He just is, that's all, and the rest he surrenders to God.

The universe will always remain a mystery to us. Even science, with all its discoveries, has yet to graduate kindergarten. The allure of the unknown intrigues the human mind, but the mind searches for answers in an objective world, a practical world where economic gain is paramount to everything else. It tries to put pieces of a puzzle together, a puzzle without solution, one that touches on eternity.

The mind is frustrated by its own inquiring nature. It forgets the inner quantity. It fears subjective foraging into realms of the unconscious. The mind needs to analyze everything, to understand the unexplainable, to reduce life to a compact equation's component parts. It rejects what it doesn't understand, and it's always at odds with itself.

Fools think they know something about life, and wise men shrug their shoulders and laugh. They look at life's beach and say, "Hey, this is terrific! I can learn something here. The water, the sand, the rain, the sky, the universe—it's all my teacher." A fool is trapped in his wisdom. He sits on a grain of sand and pontificates on the true nature of things. No one and nothing can come near him. He knows better than anyone else. He's righteous in his judgments, and he's often a caricature of himself. The answer's simple: what we know we can fit into a teacup. So it's better not to be full of oneself; it's better to spend one's life foraging in the world's mysteries.

Like Alice in her miraculous world of fantastic dreamlike creatures, we too can improvise with life; we too can step into life's whimsical dream. First we have to recognize the dream. We have to explore its limitless possibilities without trying to fit the dream into our teacup. No one in their right mind wants to swim in a tea cup, yet people, in their world-weary wisdom, in their self-indulgent righteousness, swim at breakneck speed from one end of the tea cup to the other.

There's so much emphasis today on knowing oneself, yet the self is an elusive, gnome-like creature that hoards treasure in the guise of righteousness. It changes costumes as quickly as a circus clown. I gave up long ago trying to know myself. It's a fruitless task, a boring task, a labyrinthine haze of likes and dislikes, of subtle nuances of personality, of sanity and insanity, confusion and calm, of insecurity, bloated ego and righteousness. I am not the "me" I think I am. Who am I? That's a mystery now, and I'm sure it'll be a mystery in twenty years. I'd rather surrender to God than know myself. At least I'm open to infinite possibilities. The "me" I know will swim forever in a teacup. One day it'll drown. Then what? Then what happens to the tea in the cup?

The less ego we have that clutters up our inner lives, the more room there is for spiritual energy, but people cling to anxiety and neurosis out of familiarity. They'd rather be crazy than be nothing. They'd rather hold on to tidbits of insanity than chance the void between illness and well-being. At least they know what they've got. Why chance nothingness? Why surrender? Who knows what evil demons lurk in the unknown? At least I'm familiar with my demons. They're old friends. They never surprise me.

I can take solace in my unique form of madness, and it takes guts to surrender to the unknown.

Death is the one blind spot in every human being. No one really believes it'll ever happen to them. The obituaries in newspapers are too remote for us to grasp. Unless we read a familiar name, death's a distant reality that happens to other people, not us. But life's transient affair comes and goes. No one from the seventeenth century is walking around today. No matter what we cling to, no matter what walls we build around ourselves, death's ever-present shadow turns matter into dust. The walls crumble, and our possessions are bequeathed to future generations.

History testifies to the transient nature of things, to the demise of empires, kingdoms, princedoms, fiefdoms, and demesnes. Rich and poor both inhabit six-foot parcels of land in which flesh and bones are food for worms, yet the mind refuses to dwell on nothingness. It refuses to see past death's blind spot, to recognize the illusive and temporary nature of the dream we call life. The mind rejects spirit. It refuses to accept transcendental consciousness as reality. It clings to life like a leech sucking bad blood.

We all have to learn to joyfully embrace death. We have no choice in the matter, because death is our guide into the unknown. When our consciousness connects with the infinite, both life and death disappear. They're no longer opposites, and we're finally free to dance in the arms of higher energy in the universe.

There's a line at the beginning of my short story, *Rudi: The Final Moments*, that reads, "Life should be a battlefield strewn with the corpses of our own self-images." That's essentially what spiritual work is about. It's the destruction of self-image so we can discover what's really in ourselves.

In Rudi's *Spiritual Cannibalism*, he talks about inner work being a work of self-destruction, but not self-destruction as defined in ordinary living. He means the destruction of ego, righteousness, opinionated walls and fortresses, the parts of ourselves that congest and block the flow of spiritual energy. The self is a very dangerous icon worshipped by insecure human beings, an icon divested of importance when ill health and death make their presence known, an icon in major need of restoration. The self prolongs its inane vision of life and death as long as it's blind to the transience of human existence.

Few people on this planet view life from a state of surrender. Most everyone is busy play-acting themselves, they concoct persona to bewitch and bedevil wary onlookers, they pride themselves on accomplishments that fade into the recesses of time. It's theatre at its best. At its worst, it's an absurd state brought on by absurd values adrift in a vacuum, a soap opera for the masses-- tedium, unhappiness, and people desperately trying to fill a spiritual void. There's no sense of the silent inner spiritual energy; there's no conscious plunge into rippleless pools of quiet in the human heart. Fear is so powerful it sculpts human personae. It carves out the emotional, psychological, and physical lives of people adrift in a vacuum. There's no trust, no faith in higher energy, no inner voice that guides one through the swamp. The silence "speaks" from behind a barrage of noise's false substitute for profound inner awakening. The silence threatens our house of cards. It's always there. It stares us in the face, and reflects a deep inner truth most of us fear. But in the end, there's nothing but silence. Life's absurd theatrical game gets swept away in silence. Nothing's left. Even memories fade in the minds of loved ones.

Silence is our best friend. It's the voice of God made manifest inside every human being. It's the great River Alph from Coleridge's poem, "Kubla Khan," flowing into eternity. Even loud jarring noise is part of silence. When we meditate on silence, it grows to encompass thought, sound, music, city noise; all of the above become remote gurgles in a great wellspring. We become the silence. Our words, eyes, and heart reflect the wisdom of profound silence. People ask, "What is it? What's going on inside you?" We shrug our shoulders and say, "I don't know! I really don't know! It's God! Higher energy! I really don't know." But the truth is there's nothing to know. The voice of silence rings loud in our hearts. The rest is the way of the world. The rest of life's petty concerns no longer consume our energy. We've become free of ourselves. We become a resident in the wellspring of silence.

CHAPTER TEN:

Teachers and Students

Real teachers admit they know nothing. They live in a world of paradox and contradiction, a world where ambiguity tests the quietness of a disciple's mind, where logic is defined by transcendental consciousness. It's not logic of the mind, not logic founded in contrasting points of view that vie for supremacy. The mind can't quite grasp the reality of enlightened people.

At the same time, real teachers are pragmatic. They live on the Earth and have to deal with the laws of the Earth. They function in the world and outside the world at exactly the same time. They see through the veil of illusion that surrounds conflicting ideas and opinions. They don't waste time and energy convincing anyone they're right. There's no necessity. Rightness limits them to the mind's point of view. Spiritual teachers must go beyond the mind. Their consciousness must be connected to higher energy in the universe.

People ask, "How do you learn from a guru? How do you absorb his knowledge? How do you develop similar consciousness?" One can't imitate the guru. One can learn from him, open to him, and absorb his *shakti* and use the guru's teachings to get closer to God. But each person is unique. Rudi once told me, "You can be a second-rate Rudi, or a first-rate Stuart." Whatever my limitations are, I'd rather be a first-rate Stuart than a second-rate someone else.

I never wanted to be Rudi. I wanted to be free of him by developing my own connection with God. I came to him for training. I came as a very insecure and neurotic ball of energy, a kid who played grownup in a mad world. He nurtured me. He loved me. He gave me training. He told me the marriage between teacher and student is the noblest marriage on Earth. It's a pathway to God. It's how spiritual work's been passed down from generation to generation. "Come to me in a state of surrender," he said. "Take my *shakti*. Get the strength to find your own path. Don't worship or idolize me. That'll tie me to the earth. I'm not a graven image. I struggle every day to grow closer to God. I need students because they make me work harder on myself, but I don't want to build more karma. I don't want students that tie me to the Earth."

I've seen concert pianists sit down at a piano and, with one finger touching one key, fill a music hall with the most beautiful sound. I'd wonder, "How does he do that?" If I asked him, I'm sure he'd tell me he's been practicing nine hours a day, seven days a week for the last sixty years.

Mastering the piano is easier than mastering the inner life of a human being. There's more duplicity in the mind's thought process that moves from logical answers to illogical assumptions, in a mind that ingests more energy than the body no matter how hard the body works. The training required to sing properly or play a musical instrument or professional sport is nothing compared to the training necessary to quiet the mind. A teacher provides that training. He trains his disciple in the rigors of inner work. He's a measure of his disciple's shortcomings. At the same time, he provides spiritual nourishment, *shakti*, meditation technique, and guidance. He's determined to use the master/disciple relationship to strengthen his own connection with higher energy in the universe.

A teacher has to give his teachings away. Rudi always said, "A teacher's like a cow. If a cow's not milked, it screams in pain." A teacher's no different. If he can't give his teachings away, he'll never attain enlightenment. Rudi said, "If you look up a cow's ass, you see shit." Herein lies the truth in the guru/disciple relationship. Teachers don't run popularity contests. They are what they are. It depends on what we see. It's easy to find fault with a teacher. It's very difficult to walk with him on the path to enlightenment.

Meditation practice, though seemingly esoteric in its nature, is a very practical undertaking. I do it because it works, because it helps me get closer to God. It's the only reason I practice every day. Esoterica and the occult don't interest me. More important to me is this: Is my consciousness increasing every day? Am I getting quieter inside myself, more compassionate, joyful, and happier? These are real considerations. The rest of the esoteric and occult can-can is pure diversion. It exists in an energy field far from the womb of the Mother Goddess, far from the inception of time and space. We learn about astral traveling, higher beings, both black and white magic, the bardo, astrology, Tarot, etc. These lessons have to be surrendered. They're not ends in themselves, but they're often used to manipulate people, to gain power, wealth, and position.

Most spiritual students are very innocent. They can't tell the difference between a magician and a true spiritual teacher. They're blinded by *shakti*, magic, astral emanations, the right words spoken for the wrong reasons, the demented mind games of gurus that manipulate the occult to control the lives of disciples. They're blinded by orange robes, long gray beards, soporific sensibilities that ooze phony love and kindness, promotion, advertising, communes, groups—anything they can attach themselves to for identity. They're not true disciples. They're lonely people looking for a way to escape the day-to-day difficulties of life. They're easy prey for guru-come-magicians who've tapped psychic energy and use it to play magic games with innocent seekers. The spiritual community is replete with mountebanks that sell astral dope to wide-eyed eager innocents that walk blindly into cul-de-sacs.

Rudi's work is no different. It too can be dangerous. His meditation practice channels strong psychic energy and awakens kundalini. It develops the chakra system and makes practitioners very powerful. The aroused energy can be used for megalomania, ego development, power over people, magic, occult madness, and control, anything but evolved growth toward spiritual enlightenment. It depends on what the practitioner wants.

It's dangerous to hide behind a Rudi flag. He told me many times, "If the ashram becomes an institution, I'd be the first to leave." It's not "Rudi's work" that's important; it's individuals that do the work. If they want to become magicians, if they want money, power, success, and material things, Rudi's work will accommodate them. If they want their spiritual enlightenment, it will also accommodate them. The disciple must be in touch

131

with his or her real need. Then they can benefit fully from deep meditation practice.

People ask me all the time, "Is it necessary to have a teacher?" The question makes me laugh. I wish it weren't necessary, but the mind and emotions are devious creatures that clutter our spiritual path. It takes training to master them. If students can do it without a teacher, I wish them the best. I'd love to have their secret. I'm not saying it can't be done. It's just highly unlikely. We need to be guided on the inner path. There are so many pitfalls, so many opportunities to delude ourselves. We need to take the voyage with someone who's been over the ground. A teacher prods us when we need prodding, he loves us when we need loving, and he hacks a path through our inner density, a path that ultimately leads to God. If someone can do it without a teacher, God bless them. I needed a teacher. I'm not afraid to admit it. My teacher needed a teacher, his teacher needed a teacher, and so on.

There's much cynicism today regarding the relationship between teacher and student, but that doesn't surprise me. There's cynicism about everything: politics, money, relationships, medicine, healing, food, having children, success, and power. People are inherently cynical. It took years for me to learn this. They're not just cynical about guru/disciple relationships; they're cynical about almost everything.

No one can take advantage of us unless we let them. Students and teachers who complain about each other are justified in their own minds, but the spiritual process is a process of surrender. No teacher is perfect, and no student is perfect; only God is perfect. The rest of us are struggling to find perfection in ourselves. Our thoughts obstruct the pure flow of energy between student and teacher, but surrender allows both student and teacher to learn.

Don't Worship the Guru's Hangnail

There are no perfect masters. There are only spiritually developed men and women who spend every day of their lives growing closer to God. At best, a guru is a servant. He serves his students and he serves God. If a guru proclaims his perfection, if he keeps telling you how enlightened he is, I suggest you run fast in the other direction. Often students treat their teachers like gods.

They worship the guru's hangnail. There's a difference between respect, humility, and gratitude, and a fanatical belief system that transforms a human being into God. God is God. The rest of us are evolving toward perfection. Guru worship ultimately leads to disappointment. We're bound to find flaws in the sacred cow. Without spiritual study, we flounder in a whirlpool of thought and emotion. We drift through life like dead leaves in a turbulent river. Somewhere along the line, we have to submit ourselves to somebody else's knowledge. The key to successful spiritual study is non-judgment, surrender, development of chakras, and being one-pointed in our need to get to God. Then we take from teachers exactly what we need for our own growth. When their teachings no longer work for us, we move on. Whether we agree or disagree with our teachers is beside the point. We're there to learn from them, not argue with them. We're there to take their *shakti* deep inside us, use the *shakti* to open the chakra system, and connect our consciousness with God. Everything else interferes with the spiritual process, prolongs the journey, and is like static on a radio.

In Portland, Oregon, years ago, a student of mine invited me to a Japanese tea ceremony. The man performing the ceremony, though a nice man, was obviously a novice in matters of tea. I didn't mind. The tea and companionship were good and we were all enjoying ourselves. At the end of the ceremony, he asked if anyone had a question. "Yes," I said. "Why tea?" He proceeded to discourse for twenty minutes on "Why tea?" After leaving the tea hut, I said to my student jokingly: "If this man were a master of the tea ceremony, he would've hit me over the head with a stick and said, 'Why not?'" Real teachers admit to knowing nothing. They surrender their position by giving away their teachings. They're vehicles for spiritual energy, and they teach disciples how to get free of themselves.

The question is, how does one approach a real teacher? The answer is simple: Leave all preconceptions behind. Listen, learn, keep your mouth shut, let the guru's *shakti* open chakras, be grateful, learn to serve unconditionally, trust, conserve energy, show humility and respect, and never try to imitate the teacher.

There are sects of Buddhism that talk about the necessity of "killing the Buddha." I can understand that. Rudi's energy forced

133

me to kill Stuart. I could never open deep enough to satisfy him. I'd dredge up chunks of my ego and watch him blow them to pieces. The pain of letting go is like the pain of giving birth. It's never easy. I always wanted to approach Rudi with openness and grace, but what I wanted to do often differed from my actual state of being. It was hard to leave opinion, fear, guilt, and anger at the door, but his *shakti* was strong enough to break down my ego and replace it with spiritual energy. He forgave me my lack of consciousness and guided me on the long voyage home.

The guru/disciple dynamic takes place because both surrender to higher energy. They make demands on each other, demands that force them to commit themselves to the rigorous task of being with God. Each demands the other to go deeper. It's a question of how much the guru and disciple want enlightenment. They reflect each other's tireless need to open to higher energy in the universe.

I'd often go to Rudi's store after deep meditation. He'd be busy with a client or a friend or he sat by himself. I'd hug him, then sit down on a chair next to his desk. Within minutes, my feel-good, all-purpose spiritual quiet would disappear and I'd become like a piece of burnt toast. The power of his *shakti* forced me to go deeper within myself. It ignited my kundalini. Tidal waves of energy emanated from his head and heart and navel chakras, energy so powerful it forced me to break down any image I had of myself. No defense within me could withstand the force of his *shakti*. I had to surrender everything. Often, I'd want to run. I couldn't face the shattered me being transformed into burnt toast. I'd scream at Rudi, never out loud, but a silent scream, a scream from the depths of my soul, a scream that broke open my heart and freed me from tensions hundreds of lifetimes old. I'd hug him and tell myself, I'll never be smug about meditation again. He'd look at me, smile, and then say in a playful voice, "You learn anything?" "Yes," I answered. "I love you very much. But I love God even more."

Most gurus set up protective shields around their *shakti*. They play at being perfectly enlightened masters, crystallized spiritual fat cats worshipped by wimpy, wide-eyed students. They'd rather play the role of God on Earth than give the teachings away. Rarely, if ever, do they break themselves down. Rarely, if ever, do they surrender the role of guru. There must be a guru/disciple dynamic for meditation practice to work. Both have to surrender; both have to be one-pointed in their need to find God. A disciple can have many teachers but only one root guru and no teacher is in competition with any other teacher. I've heard teachers say, "You can study only with me." When they discover their students practice other disciplines, they get righteous about the gift of *Shakti*. But spiritual disciplines don't conflict with each other. Gurus who need to control disciples are insecure gurus. They've yet to realize that God is an all-inclusive energy, that people must put all the pieces of their karma together. The mind creates conflict between different methods of practice, but it's all one, all part of life's enigmatic puzzle.

At the same time, we need one teacher to stabilize our spiritual practice. It's easy to skip like a bunny from spiritual hotspot to spiritual hotspot, but rootedness in meditation practice forces us to work deeper on ourselves. In "new age consciousness," there are too many spiritual butterflies. They're mostly frightened people with flitting needs, and they avoid confrontation with deep inner blockages. This, in itself, is a problem. It keeps them from disengaging major psychological and emotional obstacles that obstruct the chakra system.

Spiritual practice teaches that the one and the many are both one, but without the one (a root guru), the many clutters the path of spiritual seekers.

I had many teachers before I met Rudi, but his energy and teachings, his directness with life and spiritual training, his strength of purpose and ability to live what he taught, made me realize God put Rudi in my life to guide me on my spiritual path. He became my root guru. I'd studied with one baba and swami after another, in a blur of "love, peace, and eat vegetables," gurus that tried to transform a street kid from the Bronx into a *sadhu*. None of it worked for me. None of them took me deep enough to shake my neurotic self, but Rudi's bagels-and-lox, breath-and-chakra approach to kundalini yoga, his no-bullshit, day-to-day intense struggle to master himself, his lack of pretension and simple meditation practice, showed me it's possible to connect with God in this lifetime.

He was always available. At first, that came as a shock to me. Most gurus are never available. You kiss their feet between three and three fifteen in the afternoon, and then they hole up in their chambers surrounded by a cordon of spiritual heavies that isolate them from the rest of their disciples. They're like movie stars. Without the right network of connections, it's almost impossible to get close enough to them to ask a question.

After I met Rudi, I stopped looking for teachers. "Where am I going to find another person like him?" I asked myself. "Nowhere," the answer came back. "Rudi's your root guru. You've got to learn whatever he can teach."

Life's difficult with a teacher and difficult without a teacher. It's a taskmaster no matter how we live. Like Rudi once said, "Either we pay for our lives consciously or unconsciously." Whether it's hard or it's easy or it's somewhere in-between, we have to do our inner work. There's no choice in the matter. All a guru does is open pathways to enlightenment.

I know enlightenment sounds like an abstract thing, but it's really not. We start the journey to enlightenment by learning to love ourselves, then our families, friends, work and business associates and, finally, the great mass of humanity. It's a lifetime's journey. No one expects serious meditation practitioners to love humanity after the third breath. The very notion's absurd, yet we defeat ourselves because the job seems so big. We refuse to chip away at granite-like inner blocks. It could take five, ten, twenty years. It could also take five, ten, twenty lifetimes if we don't work on ourselves. Time is irrelevant. Twenty years is like a drop of water when compared to millennia. It passes very quickly. One day, we're old. The question is, "What did we do with the last twenty years? Are we happy with our lives?" If not, then twenty years slipped away without inner growth. We're still failures. We can't keep our hearts open.

It Only Takes One Person

The guru's a physical manifestation of an energy force that lives in the human heart. Only his body dies. His spirit continues to guide disciples through the rigors of life. I've never felt Rudi was gone. I don't miss him, and I don't want to drag him back to Earth. He told me many times, "If you love someone, when they die, give them the freedom to leave. Don't keep pulling them back to Earth. Build your own connection with God. Don't lament a loved one's death. He's on vacation, that's all, a rest from life's problems."

I was with Rudi when he died in the airplane crash. My first thought upon seeing him dead was, "Now, Stuart, you'll find out what the last six years were about. Now, you'll see if you got any training." I then thanked him for letting me be in the airplane, for letting me be part of his last moments. I promised him I'd never drag him back to Earth. "You live in my heart," I said to him. "You'll always live in my heart. I'm grateful for my spiritual training and for my deepening need to be with God."

When I was six years old, I'd lie in bed at night and listen to an aberrated voice in my head chant, "Rudi! Rudi!" I met him nineteen years later, but our meeting was not accidental. No meeting of a guru and disciple is an accident. Rudi lived in my heart long before my birth. He'll live in my heart long after I'm gone from here. We met for six short years. I got my training. He got his enlightenment. The rest is fantasy, folklore, and fable.

To this day, many people haven't recovered from Rudi's death. They feel abandoned, full of grief, alone, and frightened. They never got the essence of his teaching. They never worked deep enough to get real spiritual training. Now they live in faded memories of Rudi, insecure memories, a dredging up of the past's dead issue. "If you love me, Stuart," Rudi once said, "do your spiritual work in depth. Free me by getting your own connection to God."

Over the course of his lifetime, Rudi had twenty or thirty thousand students. He once told me, "All I want is one great student. That's all I need to make my life successful." One of his favorite expressions was, "throwing pearls before swine." He must have quoted it hundreds of times. But how few people understood him! How few people are ready for a spiritual life.

"All it takes is one person," Rudi said over and over, "just one disciple who's willing to serve God."

It's the guru's lifelong quest to find a great disciple, a person to whom he can give away his teachings.

Rudi never passed on his mantle, nor did he speak about successors, future Rudis, institutions, Rudra lineages, or dogmatic approaches to his work. He became Swami Rudrananda for only one reason. It enabled him to get teachings from Indian gurus.

He had to play by the rules of the game. Indian ashrams are hierarchical places with strong inner circles. Teachings are given only to those disciples close to the guru. The rest sit and chant, make flower mala offerings, receive *prasad*, and fade into the great yawn of Asia. They have the guru's grace but not the guru's personalized attention.

Rudi's stint as a swami served purely practical purposes. It enabled him to make every second of his visit to the Ganeshpuri ashram a valuable one. He divested himself of swamidom as soon as he left the ashram. He hated titles. He never gave spiritual names to disciples. His teachings weren't exclusive. Anyone could benefit from them; anyone could get close to him. He sat in his Oriental antique store eight hours a day. If you wanted to see him, if you had a question, you'd go to his store and he'd welcome you with a big smile, a hug, open arms, love, humor, a bowl of Noodles Alfredo, coffee, pecan pie, and a meditation class if he wasn't too busy with clients, friends, and relatives. He didn't fabricate mysterious veils to hide behind. He detested titles and hierarchical ranks of students basking in self-importance because they rub shoulders with their guru. He had a simple vision, that it's more difficult to be human than spiritual. He had nothing to hide. He loved God, people, and life in all its manifestations, and he wanted to taste every dish on the table.

A question I hear all the time is, "Do I have to become a teacher?" The answer is simple: no. No one has to become a spiritual teacher, but after mastering the mind and emotions, after developing a permanently opened chakra system, people start to gather around you. They're attracted by emanations of spiritual energy. They want to pull on the "cow's tits."

There's nothing a meditation adept can do about it. He or she's become a servant of God or higher energy in the universe. The process is organic. One doesn't even know when it begins, but they no longer live their own lives.

No one in their right mind wants to become a guru! It's not a job to be found at career counseling offices in college. It's more like guiding whitewater raft tours. A group of dedicated people gathers around you. You guide them through the rough-and-tumble of karma, through disturbances, around rocks and boulders, past whirlpools and eddies, over waterfalls and into calm places.

The pay's lousy, but the benefits are terrific. The work itself gets you closer to God.

If we're determined to be gurus, if we want the glitter and glitz of gurudom, if we want power over others, or boundless megalomania touching the nooks and crannies of people's minds and emotions, if control is our principal objective, whether control is a conscious or unconscious thing, gurudom turns spiritual seekers into mad kings. They find followers, like Hitler found followers, because people are attracted to neon, people who are weak and frightened and who attach themselves to groups that provide superficial safety nets, groups that use Madison Avenue techniques to promote themselves and their dogmatic vision of God. The guru's final test is whether or not he can surrender gurudom. If he can't give his teachings away, the teachings become a carapace protecting his frightened self.

After I taught my first kundalini class for Rudi at his Big Indian Ashram, he took me aside. "Next year at Big Indian," he said, "first I'll teach, then you'll teach, then we'll show cartoons." I have never forgotten those words. Rudi, me, and Donald Duck—a tripartite emission of *shakti*—a not-too-serious approach to gurudom, just another job on Earth, a way to serve God. "If I get too self-involved in my position as guru, I can always be replaced by Mickey, Minnie, or Donald," I thought.

It's best to serve God, not people. People are fickle, unreliable, insecure, and they almost always disappoint us. Their love becomes hate quicker than an actress changes costumes for her next scene. There's little or no security in most human relationships. Hidden beneath superficial expressions of love and gratitude, we often find self-serving Lilliputian types stuck in their own twisted vision of the world. Their love is lip service, a way of buying position in the guru's heart. People tell us what they think we want to hear. It's rare to find a person full of unconditional love, a person who trusts and is grateful for the gift of life, a person who can truly say thank you, a person who'll ride the whitewater raft to the end of the river.

Higher energy is another story. It's the only consistent force in the universe. If we detach our consciousness from the cesspool of mind and emotions and attach it to God, we draw upon an endless resource of nourishment. We draw upon the source of life giving birth to everything in the universe, a transcendental energy that doesn't shift and change according to moods, that's not trying to figure out the logistics of life's equation, but is there, always for us, a fountain of inner wealth that renews tired and worn bodies, unhappy minds and hearts, and our consciousness becomes an umbilical cord connected to reality not illusion.

Most problems are a result of spiritual malnourishment. People are dying of hunger and thirst. The inner sluice drips like a leaky faucet. It gives just enough spiritual energy to get us through the day. We accept the drip-drip-drip as reality. We accept neurotic minds and tumultuous emotions as the terrible joke life plays on us, a joke we can do nothing about.

On a trip to Israel, before meditation class, I made an announcement. I'd be willing to do healing sessions before class for students with real physical problems or students in need of deep spiritual growth. "If you complain to me about your parents, husbands, children, economic misfortune, etc," I said, "my fee is one hundred dollars for ten-minute sessions." Many students came before class. Not one of them dumped petty nonsense on me. Their questions were never more than a sentence long. We did deep spiritual work instead of wallowing in endless neurotic chitchat. It was very nice. The spiritual work took root in people. I grew; they grew. All of us received energy and inner strength, strength that helped resolve many life problems.

Don't Clone the Teacher

We have to learn to detach ourselves from the guru. If not, the guru becomes our limitation. No two people on Earth have the same karma. All paths are different, but detachment doesn't negate gratitude. It has nothing to do with insane Hollywood notions of walking into sunsets like John Wayne or Charles Bronson at the end of B-movies, needing no one, thinking with a sense of false independence that we are alone against the world. Even the Lone Ranger needed Tonto.

Gratitude is one of the keys to detachment. It keeps the heart open, sustains humility and love, and is a pathway to God. It's stupid to reject people who've helped us. Even if we disagree with them, even if our paths separate, gratitude helps us to move on.

It makes a place in our hearts for God. Rejection and anger do nothing but build more karma. They drain spiritual energy out of us. We can only detach ourselves from the guru by being grateful for what he has given us. Rudi's meditation work teaches detachment. One learns to substitute God for the guru, but one never stops being grateful. Rudi taught me a double-breathing meditation exercise that saved my life. How can I do anything but have love and gratitude for him? All the tales, folklore, and stories about him depend on who's telling them. They're fun to listen to, but they are not the essence of Rudi. Twenty people can tell the same story twenty different ways, but the essence of the double-breathing meditation exercise never wavers. It's an exercise that works so well on a planet where so little works. It's even freed me of Rudi. Why should I drag him back to Earth every time I meditate? He worked hard enough in his own lifetime. If God wants him here again, God will put him here, but it's not my role to deify him, complain to him, or feel sorrow because he's gone. It's my job to get my own enlightenment. The rest is up to time and evolution.

Some people have twisted Rudi's work totally beyond recognition. Others claim they've inherited the crown. There's been spiritual infighting, struggles for power—all the nonsense that follows the death of the king, all the stuff Rudi detested in his own lifetime. His picture hangs everywhere. People use it as a disguise for black magic, for megalomania, for dark occult practices, for destroying and enslaving people and other sick rituals that have nothing to do with Rudi or service to God.

I have no idea who I am, nor do I want to know. I wake up every day to the miracle of the day. What more do I have to know? I don't want a place on Earth. If I have to teach meditation practice, I'll teach until my teachings are taken away from me. Then what? Only God knows. The rest is mystery. Why live in deluded images of self? My greatest horror is to see a congregation of neophyte yogis cloned as Stuart sitting in front of me. What a terrible thing to inflict on any human being!

No student of mine can be me, nor can they inherit my throne. There is no throne! There's a simple double-breathing exercise Rudi left us. Use it and get to God. All the rest is soap opera. It builds karma and keeps us from ever becoming spiritually enlightened. No two people can experience meditation the same way; no two people will ever grow the same way. I think that's wonderful! I don't want to control anybody. I don't want to be responsible for spiritual concentration camps.

The Guru Is Not God—God Is God

Meditation class is like a health club for chakra development. We use the mind and breath to build strong *chi*, to open the heart and throat and center ourselves. We must build bridges between meditation class and the rest of life. Without bridges, the whole process falls short. We forget to take with us the essence of the meditation class. It becomes another useless experience in a chain of experiences called "our day."

Most people think meditation is like taking an adult education class. It's an interesting thing to do. Perhaps they can learn something, perhaps not, but class is class and life is life, and there's no reason the twain should meet. It's like leaving your muscles in the gym.

Meditation is not a fanatical undertaking. We don't have to live in caves, be food freaks, celibates, or be prisoners to dogma about right and wrong ways of living. We just have to sit down a half-hour a day and work inside ourselves. We have to use the mind and breath consciously.

Communes often entice people into communities where a few strong-willed individuals lord it over many weak people that hide out from life. If the commune member's chakra system isn't open, if his thoughts scream at him day and night and there's no sense of inner harmony and balance, to hide out in a commune will do him no good unless he takes meditation practice deep inside. Then it doesn't matter where he lives because the spectacle of God will be all around him.

After Rudi's death, his Big Indian Ashram, founded on high principles of spirituality, work and sharing, meditation and inner growth, became a cage full of bickering egos at odds with each other, a battlefield for mini-gurus trying to recruit disciples, a hangout for people who never truly got Rudi's teachings. Paradise transformed itself into hell. The mountains, trees, fields, and streams did little or nothing to remind people of Rudi's double breathing legacy, of his unconditional love and surrender—the reason Rudi created Big Indian in the first place.

Many people live their lives in the memory of Rudi. They've yet to let go of him. I've also heard disciples declare, "I'm the new Rudi! I've got written proof that says I'm Rudi's successor. I've inherited the throne."

The struggle for power knows no bounds. Its megalomania rips open the heart of man and eats it whole. There's no surrender, no letting go, no spirituality. Position is everything. Even swamidom is used to control other human beings. We forget we're not God. We forget God is God and the best we can do on Earth is serve God. We must free ourselves and free the people we love, and live our lives in a state of surrender. The rest of the soap opera prolongs karma. It prepares us for reincarnation. It could even bring Rudi back to Earth to clean up the mess.

I once heard a swami say, "The guru is God!" This swami spoke before hundreds of people at the Big Indian Ashram. He kept repeating, "You must worship the guru because the guru is God." The very idea of the guru being God made my stomach turn. I almost got up and left the room. Later, I heard Rudi say, "God is God. The guru is the guru! The best the guru can be is the servant of God and the servant of people that study with him." Most gurus forget this. They're so used to disciples bowing and kow-towing to them that they forget the servant's position is higher than the master's, and they begin to believe they're God incarnate. Humility disappears. The guru becomes a piece of crystal. He can never change; he can never grow, not if he's assumed the position of God. There's nowhere else to go. Remember, God is all-perfect, all-powerful, omniscient and immutable. That's quite a mantle to carry around, that's quite a reputation to live up to.

Rudi told me many times, "Don't love me; love God! Your love for me will turn to hate. It's an emotional thing, and emotions change very quickly. Don't substitute me for God."

I loved him more than any other person on Earth. Surrendering that love forced me to plummet to the depths of my being. It taught me how to let go of anything. I went through hell. Jealousy, anger, fear, and possessiveness were ripped out of me, but my love for God was more important than my love for Rudi. The former freed me; the latter would have made me an angry and bitter man.

When I finally surrendered my childish love for Rudi, the spiritual love between us became even more profound. It had nothing to do with earthly drama. Its sole purpose was to bring both of us closer to God. I often think, "That's what love is about, isn't it? People's love for each other should bring them both closer to God." It shouldn't be a possessive love, but a love based on surrender, an unconditional love shared in the light of infinite energy.

Many spiritual students have bodhisattvic complexes. They want to heal the sick and help the weak, but quasi-bodhisattvas need to develop strong inner lives. They need to work on themselves and build their own connection with God. It's easier to try to heal others than do work to heal one's self. Years ago, I surrendered my bodhisattvic complex to God. I said, "It's your problem. I can't save the world." Christ, the Buddha, Moses, Padmasambhava, and Mohammed were much more gifted than I. The world's still a mess. Their teachings did little or nothing to change things. I think time is a much better bodhisattva than I am. It can wait for eternity. It has an infinite amount of patience.

I gave up trying to heal seven billion people and worked more intently on myself. "I can help me get closer to God," I thought. "I can build Stuart. That's at least possible. The other's a waste of time and energy. Someday, my connection with God will get strong enough to affect other people, but I've got to wait; I've got to have patience. There's a Jewish expression that says, 'Save one life and you've saved the world,' but first things first. First you've got to work on yourself. The rest will follow. It's all a matter of evolution."

Years ago, in Denton, Texas, a young man with very long hair and a beard came to my shop dressed in rags. He hadn't bathed in weeks. He held a copy of Rudi's *Spiritual Cannibalism* in his hand.

"I heard that you teach Rudi's work," he said.

"Yes," I answered.

"I'd been living in the Guatemalan jungles," he went on. "I had a tent near a stream and I lived like a hermit. I meditated half the day. A stranger came and asked me if he could spend the night in my tent. He was reading this book. He gave it to me and said, 'I think this is what you're looking for.' I read the book, packed up my tent, came to Texas, and telephoned Rudi's brother in New York. He told me you taught this work. Here I am. I want to study with you." He lived in my house and studied meditation with me for four years.

When the disciple's ready, spiritual work will find him. A messenger will come. It doesn't matter if he lives in self-imposed exile. If the time's right, he'll meet his guru. A spiritual life begins, and an awakening takes place, an opportunity to study and to build a system strong enough to connect with God. When I see mixed-up and crazed looks in the eyes of people, when I see confusion and sadness, I no longer worry about it. "It's okay," I say to myself. "When the time's right, they'll find a teacher. There's nothing I can do for them now. If I preached spiritual work to them, if I lectured them on meditation practice, it would fall on deaf ears. If they're not ready to learn, nothing can perk interest. So I defer to time. It's much better at this than I am. I can only work with people who come to me. It is hard enough to teach them. It would be impossible to chase strangers in the streets." I truly believe God and time will take care of all the craziness on Earth.

Why Interfere with Wisdom?

Very few gurus are available to their students, but Rudi's work, practiced in a real way, demands availability of its teachers. They can't live in ivory towers and insulated rooms. If they surround themselves with a cordon of spiritual goons, the *shakti* will dam up inside them.

I never had a need to make conversation with Rudi. In six years together, we spent little or no time discussing various spiritual and non-spiritual subjects. I'd listen to him talk, take in his *shakti*, meditate with him, but never, not once that I can remember, did I spend time making small talk with him. I just wanted spiritual energy. I didn't care about his personal life, or his business, his likes and dislikes. I wanted to get closer to God. The rest? It held little or no interest for me. Rudi talked better than I did, anyway. In fact, he never stopped talking, but his words were not ordinary words. They were the words of a great teacher, a healer, a man of God. Why interfere with wisdom? Why put in my two cents where it wasn't needed?

It was more important for me to be Rudi's disciple than his friend. I understood that early on. He had something I wanted, and it wouldn't be given to me if I gossiped with him. People conversed with him about art, money, spiritual matters, ashrams, movie stars, and other superficial nonsense that took up his time and energy. I listened, that's all, and I learned from him, and I took in his *shakti* and tried to use him to get closer to God. Some of his students thought I was crazy, but crazy wisdom gets to the heart of a guru. I preferred to sit at his feet with humility and gratitude and absorb *shakti* than bandy about meaningless conversation with my spiritual master.

I had serious anger in me when I first met Rudi, anger so intense I never thought I'd get rid of it, anger combined with jealousy and a strong propensity for internalizing most experience. I was a time bomb in a human body. I'd scream at God, Rudi, Rudi's teachers, my friends and enemies, at anyone who'd enter my life and allow me to victimize them. But it was a silent scream, an internal scream, and I never voiced my anger to Rudi or anyone else. I kept it inside myself. I knew my victims were innocent. It was me who was crazy.

Nothing justified Stuart Perrin, a living time bomb, a victim who seethed because of his own insecurity, a frightened little big shot who knew less about life than all his targets; nothing justified me taking out my anger on someone else. I had no discipline. I had a mind that never shut up, emotions like a whirlpool of disharmonious energy, no balance, and no security. I lived like a nerve ending exposed to stimuli from all corners of life. I was the archetypal spiritual seeker who couldn't get past himself. I knew Rudi could help me. So I kept my mouth shut, sat at his feet, and tried to open my heart and take in as much spiritual energy as my system could handle. Without him, I'd be dead today.

Rudi never made life easy. Sometimes it felt like I was pledging a fraternity. I scraped and painted fire escapes, walls, lofts, and hallways, listened to him complain and argue with his mother, meditated with him, dropped tension with him, and felt his *shakti* burn to the core of my being. He taught me how to transform all my tension into fuel for a spiritual life. "You're up against yourself," he said many times. "You're angry at yourself. If you bring all that anger to the chakra below the navel, it'll help open the center of balance in you."

A disciple is less than nothing in the evolution of things, I

learned, a schmuck who thinks he's having a spiritual life, a fool
stuck on God but unable to put two sticks together on Earth.
Either he grows above it or he spends his time in terrestrial hell.
If he's smart, he uses everything to get to God, but he's still a
disciple and a disciple's prime goal is to develop chakras and keep
his mouth shut. His wisdom's a piece of dust in the wind, like
the "wisdom" of fIrst-term psychology students who play-act
Sigmund Freud.

Rudi's heart grew larger by the moment, a delicious heart filled
with boundless love and caring. He could nurture half-crazed
students, love them, have compassion for them, and teach them
how to transform their anger into spirit. He taught me not to
judge people, not to analyze them or try to figure them out. "Any
idiot can find fault with me," he said one quiet winter's day in his
store. "I'm fat...I wear orange tee-shirts...I'm a businessman...I
fight with my mother...I'm a Jew practicing Hindu/Buddhist
meditation...I like bagels, lox, smoked whitefish, roast beef, and
Sloppy Joe sandwiches. There's always something wrong. But I'm
not running for Miss America; I'm not running for most popular
guru of 1969."

There's a great deal of tension between gurus that do different types of spiritual practice. There's competition, magic, likes
and dislikes, teachers badmouthing one another, petty gossip
by ego-inflated gurus who are threatened by other gurus that
pontificate about unfamiliar forms of meditation. The politics of
gurudom are more intimidating than national and international
politics. Most disciples have no idea what's going on. They're
wide-eyed innocents who trust the orange-robed saint seated
on an altar in front of them, a saint often created from dust and
rumor, but powerful nonetheless. Often dogmatic and controlling,
he can cripple the psyche of innocent believers.

One has to choose a guru the same way one chooses food in
the supermarket: read the ingredients on the label. Don't be talked
into devoting time and effort to a work that doesn't feel right.
Listen to your inner voice. If the meditation helps you, the results
will manifest in day-to-day living. It doesn't matter if meditation
practice is difficult. Does it work? That's the important question.
If not, you spend your life clinging to fool's gold. Time passes
quickly, and spiritual enlightenment's delayed until the next

lifetime and the next lifetime and the next.

I'm Here for the *Shakti*

Samadhi (a state of enlightenment at the moment of death) is the goal of meditation practice. It's not a day of mourning; it's a day of joyful proclamation of a life well-lived, of freedom, enlightenment, and oneness with God. So when the spiritual drudge catches up to me, when I look up to heaven in disbelief thinking, "What keeps me doing this? How have I survived the last twenty years? Why not run off to a cave and forget the madness of the world?" That's when I remember Rudi's *samadhi*, and my heart opens and I'm grateful for my life. There's no price I can pay for the blessings he gave me. My tiredness, my resentment, my anger, and my restlessness are all nonsense. My neurotic self re-emerges from past karma and wants me to go backwards, but one word of thanks to my guru changes everything. It helps me go on, and it gives me the strength to survive my own demons. All the excuses become laughable. I have to serve God as best I can in this lifetime; I have to recommit myself every day to spiritual growth.

None of this is easy. Then I think, "What's easy? Nothing I know of. Nothing worth working for."

There's always conflict between guru and disciple, but not conflict in the ordinary sense of the word. They don't argue with each other. They internalize conflict and use it to break down resistance to spiritual growth.

Rudi's presence forced me to work on myself. Sometimes I hated being around him. I'd want to laze about, take my inner life for granted, be satisfied with the steps I'd already taken, but his presence, his force of *shakti*, made me see how little I'd attained, how vast a horizon I had in front of me, how easy it was to slink into ego and ego's precincts. That was enough to tempt me to make an early exit. "Who needs this?" I'd think. "I work and work; then I'm told I'm not working hard enough." "Work brings more work," he'd say a hundred times. "I'm tired of work," I'd say to myself a thousand times. "I just want to be left alone. I want to let my chakras rust, I want to let my spiritual life go to pot."

Then I'd use conflict to break myself down, to open my heart, revitalize myself, and discover I can work past my tiredness. I'd use Rudi's techniques to overcome my anger at Rudi. He was much wiser than I, both spiritually and materially, and he understood things far beyond my grasp. It didn't matter whether I agreed or disagreed with him. What mattered was spiritual growth; what mattered was getting free of myself.

I'd already been to hell and didn't like it there and nothing could induce me to go back. Trusting no one as a young man, I did what I wanted to do. Consequently, I was put in the "slammer." After I left prison, I almost committed myself to a sanatorium.

Rudi cared about me. He made a place for me in his life. That in itself inspired me to use my inner conflicts as a reason to work against myself. When I disagreed with him, I kept my mouth shut. It didn't matter to me whether he was right or wrong. Why destroy a good thing? Why interfere with the spiritual growth process? My opinions would disrupt the flow of *shakti*. They were opinions of an immature and very neurotic young man. So why bog Rudi and myself down in differences of opinion? There'd be no room for God, no room for spiritual practice. There'd be only room for disagreement. We'd fight all the time, and that fighting would destroy the guru/disciple relationship.

Rudi taught me to look for God inside people. The negative is easy to see, I learned from him. It's right on the surface, but God is hidden beneath layers of emotional and mental excrement. He's always there. We just have to find Him, and the rest doesn't matter! It's all tabloid nonsense that roosts in the minds of petty people who tear each other apart, people whose hearts are closed, who care nothing about spirit, who feed off other people's weaknesses, who must be right even if being right means destroying someone.

An hour before I left New York to live in Denton, Texas, Rudi said to me, "If anyone asks what a guru is, tell them it's life." It took ten years for me to understand what he meant, but, finally, I realized the guru is consciousness. It's the spectacle of life that manifests around me, that teaches me exactly what I have to learn to get close to God. All I have to do is listen, be grateful, open my heart, quiet my mind, and let the guru guide me on the path.

I never fought with Rudi—never. Not for a moment did I express opinions of right and wrong to him. I surrendered them. I used them to deepen my own inner work. His personal life was none of my business. His business, family, love affairs, tastes in food, people, art, and literature were none of my business. I reminded myself over and over again, you're with him to get *shakti*. His *shakti* is essential for your life. You're like a child on mom's nipple, I thought. A child has no opinions. It drinks its mother's milk. That's all! It doesn't judge the mother. It takes in her milk and it lives.

Neither the guru nor disciple can judge each other. Their opinions have to be surrendered for the sake of spiritual growth. Any situation, be it an ashram, commune, church congregation, or schoolroom, will have politics, in-fighting, likes, dislikes, gossip, and micro groups that vie for self-interest. None of that concerns a true disciple. He's there for one purpose—to get the guru's *shakti*. If he forgets his one-pointedness and joins the circus of baboons that play spiritual politics at the ashram, his connection with the guru will vanish. Personality comes into play, but *shakti*, the necessary transmission that feeds a deep inner need, can never become mind prattle, political maneuvering, or any kind of distorted version of what it means to give and receive.

One can never forget that one studies with a guru to get spiritual training. Every guru has different demands, but the bottom line is always whether or not guru and disciple are growing spiritually. That's a precious truth. The rest is fodder for the compost heap.

After Rudi died, I went to India and met a Tibetan teacher named Kalu Rinpoche with whom I visited three times in three days. The meeting turned out to be one of the most remarkable experiences of my life. In fact, it was so remarkable that the meeting became legend in Kalu Rinpoche's Tibetan Buddhist community.

He lived in Sonada monastery just outside of Darjeeling. Two Tibetan lamas took a student of mine and me to meet Rinpoches in monasteries in and around Darjeeling. When we came to Sonada monastery, scores of burgundy-robed Tibetan lamas sat in the yard. We asked to see Rinpoche.

"He's not well," one of the lamas said to us. "He's not seeing anybody."

"Maybe he'll see us," I said. "We've come from far. Can you go ask him?"

The lama went inside. He came out with a surprised look on his face. "Rinpoche will see you," he said. He then took us to Kalu Rinpoche's quarters.

Rinpoche lay in bed with the covers up to his neck. He had an ascetic, sweet old face with large, black, compassionate eyes—a beautiful face, now pale and sallow. He looked like he was ready to leave the world. We sat down at his feet. By way of a translator, he greeted us. He asked our names, where we came from, and then he talked about Tibetan Buddhism and Tibetan Buddhist lore. Both my student and I sat at his feet in a state of deep meditation. When he finished, I asked him if we could return tomorrow. He said, "Yes."

The next day, when we entered his quarters, Rinpoche was sitting cross-legged in robes on his bed. Once again, we sat down at his feet and began to meditate. He talked for well over an hour. When he finished, I asked him, "Can we come back and see you again tomorrow?" He said, "Yes."

As we walked out of the monastery, my student told me he once read a book on Tibetan Buddhism that spoke about *tummo*, one of the Six Disciplines of Naropa, a form of Tibetan Buddhist meditation very similar to our meditation practice. I thanked him. I now had questions to ask Kalu Rinpoche.

The next day, when we returned to Rinpoche's quarters, he was sitting cross-legged in full teaching regalia on a throne chair. We sat down at his feet. "Rinpoche," I asked. "Could you please talk about the Six Disciplines of Naropa, specifically the discipline of *tummo?*"

Rinpoche spoke for three hours on all facets of Tibetan yoga. He gave us a complete Tibetan Buddhist education. At the end of his discourse, he stopped talking for a moment. Then he said, "When I was a young *tulku* in Tibet, if I wanted to see my Rinpoche, I'd have to wait on line for three hours. Many lamas had questions about their spiritual lives. There were great lines in front of my Rinpoche's quarters. Today, I have to look for people to teach."

Hundreds of lamas sat in the Sonada monastery courtyard. They turned prayer wheels, counted *japa* beads, but not one of them understood the true nature of Rinpoche's illness. He was the proverbial cow that needed to be milked, a teacher who needed to give his teachings away. Students must make a conscious effort to receive teachings from their guru. If they don't milk the cow, the cow's tits dry up. The cow will shrivel up and die. So God sent my student and I to Kalu Rinpoche. We came from Texas to "milk" an underused Tibetan Rinpoche. The translator told me that in thirteen years of living in Rinpoche's monastery he had never heard the teachings Kalu Rinpoche gave to my student and I.

About twenty years ago, in San Francisco, another student of mine met a Tibetan Buddhist practitioner, a close follower of Kalu Rinpoche. He told my student a strange tale that became legend in their monastery. "It was 1975," the man said. "Rinpoche was dying. Two seekers came from the west to sit with Rinpoche. Their hunger for a spiritual life was so strong it drew out of Rinpoche teachings that not only gave them life, but Rinpoche as well. They healed Rinpoche of a serious illness."

CHAPTER ELEVEN:

Relationships

Relationships can be long-term, healthy, loving, delicious, nurturing, and full of joy if the people involved with them have independent connections with higher energy in the universe, if people involved do not live off each other's vital energy. When romance dwindles, when the sex isn't as scintillating as before, when relationships become day-to-day work, few, if any, of us have resources to keep them creative.

A spiritually starved populace needs food to keep it alive. Without energy, it dries up, but almost no one has real spiritual training. People don't know how to open chakras, how to breathe properly, how to stay balanced and keep the heart from closing up. They don't know how to sustain a connection with God. They live off each other's energy. It's a form of unconscious vampirism, a desperate effort to feed a starving soul.

The mind's frenzied voice cries out for nourishment. It's like the man-eating plant in the film *Little Shop of Horrors* that keeps screaming, "Feed me!" The mind's endless well consumes the energy of people we love. It feeds off of life's less fortunate, be it our mate, children, friends, or business associates. The mind's predatorial feeding frenzy won't stop until we learn to keep it quiet. But if we love ourselves, if we're grateful for our lives, if we feel self-worth, our tension is reduced to a manageable frequency. Loneliness disappears. We no longer desperately seek mates.

Most neurotic tendencies are a byproduct of spiritual malnourishment. If people are happy, they find little or nothing wrong with life. For example, when we fall in love with someone, we forgive them almost anything. We're compassionate, helpful, blind to their faults, and willing to help them work through problems. We cook dinner for them, serve them, wash dishes for them, and share in household chores. Nothing is too much or too little. It's later, when the love simmers, when the passion dies down, when the drudgery of the relationship becomes manifest, that we discover the faults of others, the things we like and dislike. Then we're less forgiving, more argumentative, and starved for affection. When the heart's closed, it's easy to see what's wrong with people. It's easy to complain about life's injustices.

Malnourished people need to eat. Confusion of mind and emotions drives them to cannibalize each other. They've no connection with higher energy, no spiritual life, so they weave mental and emotional spider webs to catch prey, to feed themselves with whatever food unsuspecting partners are willing to provide. It's no different than the jungle. It's a virtual feeding frenzy of lost souls that try to draw love in whatever form it takes.

Those fortunate souls who work deeply on themselves, who develop strong inner lives and a connection with higher creative energy in the universe, those souls plugged into spirit, who have no need to cannibalize loved ones, who have independent connections with God—those fortunate souls can share happiness, love, joy, and gratitude with people close to them. They're not spiritually malnourished. Their minds are quiet, their hearts open, and there's inner balance. They recognize human error to be part of life's design. They can forgive partners, have compassion, and recognize drudgery as part of life's day-to-day process. More importantly, they regenerate their own lives by deepening their connection with God. They don't have to live off their partner's energy. Find two married people that work deeply on themselves every day, and you'll probably find a healthy relationship.

Confusion runs rampart. There are so many kinds of relationships and so few people doing profound meditation work. There are parents, bothers, sisters, husbands, wives, business and work associates, cousins, aunts, uncles, and other relationships ad infinitum. Each person brings baggage into our lives, but few people bring joy and love. If we approach relationships intelligently, they remind us we have to get stronger. If other people refuse to change, there's nothing we can do about it. No lecture, no verbal pontification, no encomium or speech on spiritual living is going to dent their well-developed carapace. We discover there's only one real option, to work on ourselves and to grow spiritually every day. The rest is wind blowing nowhere.

If our hearts are open when we're alone or in a crowd, if we can "lean and loaf" and meditate on a blade of grass, if we can love ourselves and others, if we're one of those rare souls who are happy and we can share joy with others, in all probability, we can succeed at relationships. We can also succeed without relationships. We can relate to a tree, the wind, a bird, the silence in our own hearts, the noise on the street, and tension in other people. Nothing throws us for a loop.

Many relationships are byproducts of loneliness. Another person pays attention to us, courts us, makes a dinner for us, takes us to a movie or a play, and sends flowers. That person draws us out of our shell, makes us feel wanted, replaces loneliness with companionship, and pulls us into a relationship. We think it's better to be with someone than to be alone. But the magic wears thin, and often, two people draw apart. They no longer feel connected, but live together out of habit, not because of love and spiritual commitment. There's a dry, world-weary acceptance of companionship rather than loneliness. People talk at each other and not to each other, and love, that sweet nectar that nurtures deep parts of our being, so essential for life, dries up like a riverbed in a draught.

For a relationship to be fresh, both parties must recreate themselves every day. They must find new parts of themselves to share with loved ones. The old emotional two-step stops working. It grows stale. Personality exhausts our partner, but a fresh, deep regeneration of self, a newness shared with our beloved, a rekindling of the heart chakra, a love that has the sparkle of a newborn baby, all are byproducts of deep spiritual work. As we tap new resources of creative energy in ourselves, we share them with loved ones. It takes great strength and vitality to do the above, strength built over years of inner work, strength born out of one's connection with higher energy in the universe.

Nearness is not the key to love, nor is possessiveness or jealousy. It takes great strength and inner security to give another person the freedom of their life. Why suffocate them with ego?

Why snuff out their creative energy?

No one on Earth is our possession, not in life's transient and fleeting quickness where jealousy's the quickest way to lose a lover. Fifty years of marriage to a jealous husband or wife means nothing. It's just time badly spent. The marriage most likely lost its spark long ago. The rest is play-acting. People live together for the sake of the children. There's no heart connection, no love, no real joy, nothing but empty movement, dry, dead kisses, robotic lovemaking, fifty years of unhappiness, and the constant fear of loneliness. Jealousy's hellish aura sucks the creative juice from love's core. It makes prisoners out of human beings.

Trust is a prime ingredient in healthy relationships, trust and giving one's partner the freedom of their life. We can't control them anyway. It's a waste of time and energy. If our lives are creative and full of real joy and we're not dependent on other people to fill vast spaces inside us, then there's no problem trusting. Even if our partner deceives us, nothing is lost except a deceiving partner, a person we should never have married in the first place. There may be separation with all its legal and practical problems, but our hearts are still full of joy and gratitude. We're not dependent on anyone else to make us happy.

My early years with Rudi dredged up deep jealousies I never knew were there. I discovered a mysterious creature that lived in shadowlike caverns remote from my consciousness. It crept into my mind and emotions and then refused to leave. It took years of meditation practice to rid myself of jealousy. I finally grew past it. It became a tiny particle among many particles of consciousness, a dangerous one, but one I managed to keep quiet.

Jealousy destroys many relationships. It's a disease few partners can cope with, a disease that lingers and grows and takes over like weeds in a garden. We've got to pay strict attention to this disease. We've got to work deeply in ourselves until we're free of it, until a strong chakra system can transform jealousy into spiritual energy. It's a deep-rooted emotion that stems from childhood insecurity. It doesn't just go away. But there's no easy cure. It takes years of inner work to clean out jealous emotions because they cling to us like barnacles to the bottom of a ship.

Life becomes bearable when we bring joy to relationships, when our hearts are open and we offer unconditional love to students, friends, and family. At all other times, it's a struggle to survive the day.

There are no easy relationships. At least, I've never seen or experienced one. That may be my own reality. I don't know, but relationships test the resolve of most people. When they make us go deep within ourselves to gather energy and grow closer to God, they serve a very real purpose. They assist us on the path to spiritual enlightenment. We should be grateful to our partner and learn from both the positive and negative aspects of relationships. Too often, we use them to defeat ourselves. If they bust our ass, so what? Most of life busts our ass anyway; most of life's a tightrope that spans perilous cliffs. If we happen to be married to Count or Countess Dracula, then a quick exit defeats nothing but a wrongfully-made marriage. Why hold on to something that's killing you? Masochism does nothing but destroy the masochist. It eats out the core of one's being.

There's no shortage of love-starved, willful, lonely, empty, and frightened people that live like vampires on the rest of mankind's energy. They don't know how else to function. The idea of God and spirit draws a blank in them. They're not ready to listen to thoughts on deep meditation; yet, in their own way, these people are teachers. If nothing else, they teach what not to do. We find them in business, politics, families, and friendships—in almost every area of life. You cannot avoid them. They're like mosquitoes on a warm, muggy summer's night. No matter how many you swat, there are still hundreds of them buzzing about. It's easy to complain about their behavior but difficult to keep them at bay.

We need patience, forbearance, a thick skin, and a heart of gold. We need inner strength to ward off their attacks. It's like Christ said, "Forgive them, they know not what they do." But forgiveness doesn't mean permissiveness. It doesn't mean we let vampire types cling to us. We can say no to them. They don't have to leech off our energy.

If a person's trying to change, if they work on themselves every day, if confusion forces them to make more of an effort, and if they have the guts to fight for their lives, then craziness is not a factor. I've never met a sane person. It's almost as if life's designed that way. It's almost as if we have to struggle for anything of value. Why should relationships be easy? What's easy in life? Nothing worth attaining is easy, nothing we treasure, nothing we hold dear. Even mediocrity takes its toll. It atrophies chakras and transforms us into petrified humans.

Many students of mine are married to spouses uninterested in meditation practice. They often ask me how to deal with unconscious husbands or wives, how to make their relationships better. I tell them patience is the key. They have no choice but to work deeply on themselves, get stronger, and patiently wait for their partner to become aware of a higher power. No one's going to change immediately. If you force-feed them meditation, they're going to vomit it back in your face. I tell them to fasten their seat belts, build deep inner strength, love their partners unconditionally, keep looking for the positive side of things, and prepare themselves for the ride. Time brings great changes even to the thickest of spouses.

CHAPTER TWELVE:

Service

If service is an extension of our inner life, if it's an unconditional offering of deep love, compassion, and gratitude, then service becomes an important way to work out karma on Earth. If it's philanthropy, it reeks of graft. It's a way to buy God's good graces, a way to build an image of oneself, to get tax relief, and to promote oneself as a money-spending good guy who gives less a shit about people, than about his own projected image on life's screen. Service must be unconditional. It's got to come from the heart, not from the mind that projects false images of good guys at work in the world. Sadly enough, we're dominated by the false good-guy image. Philanthropy dominates the mindset of charitable organizations that stalk big spenders like Indian braves once stalked buffalo.

We need service in the world. We need to learn to actively surrender on Earth, and we need to learn that unconditional giving is essential to the evolution of spiritual consciousness. True service is a state of grace few people understand. If service comes from the center of the heart, the person that serves is awash in love. They're grateful for life, for the very breath of life, for the opportunity to have a spiritual life, and that gratitude manifests as service. It's hard to say thank you when the heart is closed.

Guilt compels possessive people to give. This has little or nothing to do with unconditional love. It's a way to control people, to satiate deep feelings of insecurity in the giver. Parents control children by reminding them all the time, "Look what I've done for you." They suffocate the true creative spirit in a child. They control

159

the child by toying with the child's intangible feelings of guilt. It's the "Eat! Eat!" don't-tell-me-there's-never-been-food-on-the-table syndrome. It forces the child to hate the food he's putting in his mouth. We can't stuff our goodness down other people's throats. They resent "goody-goody" practice that doesn't come from the heart. It's an overbearing, almost detestable cover for weakness and insecurity. It makes children shudder. They grow up resenting people who want to help them.

Quite frequently, parents relive their own lives through their children. They sacrifice themselves so the child has opportunities the parents never had. The parents learn unconditional love and surrender, a healthy lesson if the child doesn't have to live up to images parents have of them, if the child can breathe, if the child doesn't become a little animal stuffed with guilt, and if the child finds his own creative path through life. All a child needs is love. The rest is a poor extension of a parent's insecurity. It's foolish to think we can live our lives through our children. It's the quickest way to destroy them.

Unconditional giving is the heart's extension of love and gratitude made manifest in the world. The giver has no preconceived expectations. He gives because it's a joy to give. He serves because service is a path to God. It's one-half of a necessary circle that completes his humanity. The other half is unconditional receiving. Both are nonjudgmental. Both have nothing to do with philanthropic strings that make puppets of charities on the receiving end. They're expressions of gratitude, simple and loving, and they give life instead of creating prisons woven from threads of guilt. We're all given the gift of life. It's a pure, unconditional gift tainted by the world's never-ending stream of judgment. Innocence disappears at an early age, and the rest of life's a struggle to return to the Garden of Eden.

Years of meditation practice inculcate new methods of witnessing life. We become less afraid of surrender, more willing to give unconditionally, and more understanding of the spiritual process. There's nothing to lose and nothing to hide. We no longer set up impenetrable defense mechanisms to protect our valued ideas. We listen with an inner ear and see with an inner eye. Giving is a joy. It demands responsibility, consciousness, a less opinionated, more creative way of living. It demands compassion, forgiveness, love, joy, and unconditional receiving.

Rarely, if ever, do people feel responsible to anything in life but themselves. They follow the guidelines of mind and ego. "It's mine," they scream at life, "and I'll do anything to get it. The world be damned! I'll clear swamps and forests and pollute the atmosphere. I'll murder and steal and promote violence and sell drugs. It doesn't matter. As long as I get mine. That's it! That's all I care about!" There's little or no responsibility. To serve the mind is to serve one's own view of the world. No two people alive have the same view. There's always conflict, war, oppression, and other ego-induced malfeasance that causes suffering on Earth. Unconditional service seems futile when compared to the dictates of mind and ego.

When we serve higher energy, we take full responsibility for our lives, karma, the planet we live on, our homes, families, friends, and jobs. It can't be done without deep inner strength. Life's a good reminder that to give and to receive unconditionally are important if we're to live here like human beings.

Stuart Perrin

CHAPTER THIRTEEN:

Karma and Reincarnation

Human beings rev up their egos and drive full throttle toward dead ends. They do it over and over again, rarely, if ever, do they learn to drive on streets that connect to other streets. When they're finished testing all of life's dead ends, they come to realize nothing frees them except deep spiritual work. They've arrived at a place where they're ready for meditation practice. The merry-go-round comes to a halt. It's their last incarnation, their last tap dance on life's stage. They've learned all the lessons to be learned, and they're on the path that leads directly to infinite energy in the universe.

No one can learn Earth's full curriculum in one lifetime. The human soul evolves through many levels of consciousness, each a teacher in a different department at the university, each an ingredient in the spiritual cake. It's just as important to learn what not to do as it is to learn what to do. We're given many lifetimes to get our education. The soul evolves and changes and wears sundry costumes until it masters the ultimate lesson, to surrender to God, enlightenment, and oneness with higher energy in the universe.

Most people don't believe in reincarnation. They want tangible proof, scientific evidence, cold-hard facts. It's not my job to give it to them. It's my job to follow the guidance of my own inner spirit, to open to all life's possibilities and use them to get closer to enlightenment. There's so much mystery, so much that transcends human comprehension, and so much to learn. Life's mystery lends credence to reincarnation. Without it, we live in a hopelessly absurd place, a setting from a Jean-Paul Sartre novel.

There's no exit. Existence is pain and suffering without purpose. People are like marionettes controlled by political and sociological strings. Only matter evolves. The soul of man dies when man dies. Life and death do battle, but life never wins. There's nothing on Earth but hopelessness and absurdity. The individual doesn't exist. At best he's part of a greater whole, a congregation of other human beings that move full throttle toward nothingness. We might as well blow the Earth up now. What purpose does it serve if each person is no more than a part of a puzzle, if each person lives in futility, if each person's trapped in a labyrinthine network of half-crazed thoughts and ideas terminated by blessed death?

The Earth is populated by newly-born souls, very old souls, and everything in between. No two souls on Earth are exactly alike. Each is in a different stage of evolution. Each is confronted by its own particular dead end.

Earth's university keeps evolving souls busy. It teaches a vast curriculum called "Life," and each soul must study the curriculum. Each soul must prepare itself to surrender to God. Intense pain, trauma, and suffering eventually bring people to this realization. They become conscious of futility, of the dream we call reality, of illusion in all its myriad forms, all of which forces us to do something about ourselves. Time gives us many incarnations to learn to make conscious use of our suffering. We don't have to rush into it. When the soul's mature enough to begin deep meditation practice, when there are no more excuses, when there are no more dead ends to crash into, when money, fame, and success lose their luster, when we've finally had a taste of God, it's all enough to keep us working on ourselves the rest of our lives. We're ready to free ourselves of endless rounds of pain and suffering.

Karma changes as the soul evolves and grows in life's university, but karma's not limited to subjects studied. It's also a mirror that reflects one's inner self. When we look in that mirror, we discover the true nature of our soul. The mirror becomes an ally in the never-ending struggle to transcend ego, opinion, and judgment. But we can't change its reflection without changing in ourselves. If a mirror reflects a pimple on our nose, the pimple's not going to disappear because we clean the glass. Karma's no different. It's both the pimple and the reflection of the pimple, the act of getting rid of the pimple, and the smooth skin when the pimple is no longer there. Karma's whatever happens to us in life. It can change consciously or unconsciously. That depends on the evolution of each individual soul.

Meditation practice builds harmony and balance in the practitioner. This affects karma. If the mind and emotions are quiet, if we feel love for ourselves, if we're happy and full of gratitude, then our karma will reflect a spiritual path. There are fewer barriers between God and us. We're not afraid to change, nor are we afraid to resurrect the spiritual child buried deep in our unconsciousness. We have patience with ourselves and with other people. We're too busy enjoying the miracle of creation to be distracted by life's petty soap operas. We witness cycles that complete themselves. We realize life and death live together in the same seedling. One cannot exist without the other. The mirror's reflection tells us exactly what we must do to unite with God. Meditation practice helps us see ourselves more clearly in the mirror, which serves our conscious evolution and eventual enlightenment. More simply put, if we know what's wrong, we can fix it.

Most people try to fix the image in the mirror by dressing it in different clothing. They blame the reflection for their problems. If they lived somewhere else, had another car, another profession, more money, a better TV, or another mate... They're always changing the outer manifestation. Rarely, if ever, do they go inside themselves and assume full responsibility for their lives.

The moment we're strong enough to admit we're wrong, the magic mirror of karma reveals basic truths. It shows us the source of the problem. If we no longer have to defend our ego, if we're not afraid of vulnerability, of being hurt, of looking foolish in other people's eyes, we'll get to the source of the problem in ourselves and change it.

We Need Spiritual Smarts

Karma teaches the mystery of death and rebirth, of cycles that persist, of cycles that complete themselves, of the known and the unknown dancing a two-step into eternity. The soul transmigrates from lifetime to lifetime while the universe patiently waits for us to learn to read karma's magic mirror. The ego that thinks it knows better than the magic mirror interferes with the process. It creates barriers for us to overcome; it creates conflict between ourselves and the reflection we see in the mirror. We've got to develop spiritual smarts. We've got to realize the mind and emotions trick us into believing illusion is reality. They trick us into believing the pimple we see in the mirror can be removed by wiping the glass.

People prolong suffering by refusing to change within themselves; by clinging to relationships that no longer work; to jobs that bore them; to TV programs that dull their minds; to repetitious books, movies, and social gatherings; to junk food, alcohol, and cigarettes; and to other habits too numerous to list. They deny themselves access to a vast inner world of transcendental energy. They reincarnate over and over until they see their own reflection in karma's mirror, until the guru/disciple relationship becomes clear to them, until the ego is silenced and they learn to apply deep meditation practice to daily living.

We're given teachers on Earth as well as in heaven, teachers that can help us work out karma, but to live in the guru's grace without doing deep spiritual work is an insult to the guru. The "disciple" uses the teachings cheaply. He's part of the crowd *pranam*-ing at Baba's feet, but the crowd rarely, if ever, lives in Baba's heart. To get into his heart, we've got to work deeply within ourselves. There's no hiatus, no shortcut, nothing but one's need to be with God. Then we transform need into enlightenment.

There's a teacher for every human being. When the soul evolves to a mature state, when mind and ego no longer dominate one's inner being, when the heart longs for spiritual awakening, the teacher appears and guides his disciple into realms of higher consciousness. This could take hundreds of lifetimes.

Most teachers have an assortment of students. Some disciples are ready to do deep spiritual work. Then there are younger souls that touch upon spirit realms for the first time. Their commitments are less formidable. They are mostly part-time yogis. They drift with other currents, then come back for a taste of spiritual energy, and then drift again. They're not, as yet, ready to make deep commitments.

A teacher must have patience with drifters. He plants seeds in them that will grow in future lifetimes. Their karma doesn't allow them to commit to spiritual enlightenment. They need to learn about money, marriage, family, worldly success, etc. Often, they need to find other teachers to help them on the path. No teacher is right for everyone. It's the height of ego to think one can enlighten armies of people. It's a miracle to find one great disciple. Both Christ and the Buddha had a handful of disciples. Institutionalized religion came later. It was developed by less-enlightened masters.

It's difficult to commit to spiritual practice if one isn't ready, but if we study with a guru, why not learn what he has to teach? Even if we're just passing through, why waste time? Why resist something that may help us in our lives? I passed through Kalu Rinpoche's monastery. In just three sessions with him, I received teachings that helped me on my path. I never sat with him again. Most of the monks in his monastery had not received the teachings I received in just three sessions. He's not my root guru, but he'll always live in my heart.

Get Serious about Spiritual Work

People live behind masks carved from personality and deep tension. We can only guess what goes on when they're by themselves, when the masks come off and they look into karma's mirror. We can only guess what people think when they scrutinize their naked selves. There must be great fear and trembling.

It's rare to find people who are happy all the time, and their personalities do a poor job covering up insecurity. It's like bad restoration, like veneered furniture in the weather. Personality peels away in front of karma's mirror, and pretense lasts only as long as the surface keeps from crumbling.

Nobility of soul manifests when the heart's open during periods of duress. It's easy to be happy after winning the lotto, but few, if any of us, feel gratitude when times are difficult. The heart's fragile nature strengthens with resolve. It's defeated only if we let it be defeated. We can always blame defeat on karma. At the same time, karma can uplift us, help us embrace higher consciousness, and teach us ways to free ourselves from ourselves. It all depends on how deeply we work on ourselves every day. When we combine joy with responsibility, the cycles of karma come to a screeching halt.

Karma shifts and changes as we change inside ourselves. It's not a stagnant force. I remember saying to myself at age twenty-five, "Get serious about spiritual work. If you don't, there's only one path you'll be able to take, and it's not going to lead to God." I met Rudi a few weeks later. Karma brought him into my life. I applied his teachings to my life and I realized that it's impossible to change my karma, but it's possible to change myself. Then my karma will guide me all the way to spiritual enlightenment.

We bring karma into the world and we take karma from the world, but karma shouldn't negate the desire to work. It should inspire us to go deeper in ourselves, to open more, to get off life's funny little merry-go-round.

Most people give up on spiritual work when the going gets a little tough. They can't get past their minds and emotions. They'd rather dilly-dally in life's confusion than use their minds and breath to tap vast resources of spiritual energy. Often, I hear, "It's karma! What's the point! It's all predetermined, anyway." In truth, there is no point in deep inner work other than freeing oneself from oneself. If a person can't see this, there's no point trying to explain it to him. It would be like talking Greek to a Chinese person. Nothing makes sense but the mind's interpretation of reality. Then it's a question of evolution. We hear, see, and understand what we're ready to take in. The rest is gibberish.

It's impossible for the rational mind to understand how karma works. Its mystery is hidden in being. If we live our lives in the moment, there's no necessity to understand karma. We are, that's all, and the rest can be interpreted by theologians and philosophers. Nature doesn't understand itself. It exists in the moment. It doesn't have to know "why, how, or what?" Explanations are unnecessary. Nature has transcended rational mind and logical understanding. It's a living entity that cares nothing about yesterday or tomorrow.

The moment is all we have. When we accept that, when we learn to extricate ourselves from the clutches of yesterday and tomorrow, when we realize the past is dead and the future is today unfolding itself, we've attuned our consciousness with karma. We no longer think about life. We live it consciously. All the rest leads to dead ends. If we live fully in this moment, the future will take care of itself.

As a young man, I worried a great deal about the future, and today I am in the future. I could have saved so much time and energy if I had not worried. All that energy could've been used to build the present, but I wasn't strong enough to stay centered. It took meditation practice to quiet my mind, to get me centered, and teach me to live in the moment. I stopped worrying about what's behind me and what's in front of me. I do my life now, and the future unfolds in a miraculous way. What more do I have to know? If I live in the moment, the rest is illusion.

Does worrying about the future do any good? Career, family, age, and death—all of it is fabricated by nervous minds. The present offers golden opportunities. Whatever our job, whatever our family situation, whether we have a spouse, a boyfriend or girlfriend, whatever our life is at this moment, we should be grateful it's our life and try to live it as fully and happily as possible. We're no more or less than what our life is in the present. Why be unhappy with it? Why struggle against ourselves? To accept the present helps free us from our karma. To fight it is to create more karma, more reasons to reincarnate, more difficulty and tension.

Life and death are married to the human soul. One doesn't exist without the other, and the soul, almost as mysterious as death itself, links the unknown with the known, and bridges a void that separates the finite with the infinite. The soul evolves through time and space. It's the seat of consciousness, the sleeping cobra at the base of the spine, the link in the chain between being and nothingness. There's much the soul has to learn on Earth, and it spends many incarnations completing its education. Once it graduates, the soul moves on to other planes of consciousness. There, it continues its education and continues to do the work of God.

Meditation practice enlightens the practitioner to the soul's evolution, a process that often takes considerable lifetimes before coming into fruition. The soul must free itself of karma to evolve to higher planes. It's a sleepy soul, coiled up and recumbent at the base of the spine, awaiting the meditation practitioner's use of mind and breath to free it to rise and connect with higher energy in the universe. The marriage of the human soul and the universal soul gives birth to an energy force that transcends the limitations of time and space.

The universal soul is without limitation. It's connected to God and to the soul of each human being. It has been said, "The body is the temple of God." Each chakra is an altar in this temple. Each is connected to the spine, and the spine is the only place in a human being where energy rises, where the human soul evolves and connects with God.

We are the limitation—our minds, our emotions, our physical bodies, our will, our lack of balance, our priorities, where desire takes us, and the things we identify with. Our day-to-day activity reflects how evolved we are. The moment we desire someone or something on Earth, be it success, marriage, objects, money, or a spiritual life, we have to prepare ourselves for the repercussions of desire. We have to remember joy and suffering dance to the same repetitive tune. They are a byproduct of desire. One gives birth to the other. I can't remember a positive experience not being followed by a negative experience. The reverse is also true.

As long as we desire worldly possessions, there will be pain. Even the desire for enlightenment attracts pain. Yet we're born on Earth, we live on Earth, and we have to work out karma. The inevitable pain of living must be transformed into spiritual energy. If desire brings pain and the lack of desire also brings pain, there's no sense complaining about mishaps, mistakes, disease, and obstacles. We can't escape life's perplexing whirlpool of suffering. We can only use it to get closer to our spiritual enlightenment.

CHAPTER FOURTEEN:

Testing a Spiritual Life

Meditation class isn't the real gauge of a spiritual life. When we leave class, when we interact with ordinary events in day-to-day life, we discover quickly how centered we are, how open we are, how connected we are to God. We discover whether or not we've built a bridge over the void that separates meditation class from daily events. Class is easy. The energy's strong, people are open, and we're focused on spiritual practice. But at home, on the job, and at school, when we interact with tense people, we immediately discover how much centeredness we bring with us from class.

It is difficult to breathe properly in class, to focus the mind, to stay centered, and to keep the heart open. It is difficult to work against ourselves and trust that God will guide us on the spiritual path. And it is difficult to keep the mind quiet forty-five minutes, but the difficulty of meditation class pales in comparison to interacting with unconscious people.

For instance: Your coworker's chewing big wads of bubble gum and smoking her twentieth cigarette. She's spitting on the floor and complaining about everyone in the office. Your boss is screaming and farting and grumbling and tensely waiting for an important telephone call. Your sister's broken up with her boyfriend, and your mother's blamed you for sixty things wrong at home. The taxi driver almost gets you killed, and the waiter drops a glass of red wine in your lap. You feel your energy being drained out of you. You're tired and want to sleep, but it's humid and hot and you've got a rotten taste in your mouth.

Daily inconveniences test our patience, our fortitude, our

ability to stay centered and deal with life in a calm way, but we can use them to gauge spiritual progress, to find out whether or not we've built a bridge that connects meditation class with the rest of life.

We work in meditation class to break down inner blocks and create a direct link between ourselves and infinite energy in the universe. But the class ends, and we've got to go home. The quiet, joyful energy of class is then tested by unconscious people in all walks of our lives. It is not that they do it deliberately. They just do it! They're time bombs that explode over nonsense. They're always present. They're a force we have to deal with.

Meditation practitioners become bridge builders that connect the power of spiritual work with all facets of life. Meditation doesn't end when class is over. It's a twenty-four-hours-a-day process. Just as we take our muscles with us when we leave the gym, we also take our chakras with us when we leave meditation class. We don't leave them on the prayer rug.

Meditation class is a useless experience if it can't be applied to the rest of life. We have to learn to deal with people in a simple way. We have to learn to be grateful for a glass of water, a flower, our bed, the food we eat, the clothing we wear, and whatever's given to us in the course of a day. Why let unconscious people strip us of our connection with God? Why treat meditation class cheaply? Because someone else is crazy, it doesn't mean we have to be crazy.

Within five to ten minutes of leaving meditation class, something will manifest to test our resolve. Life is full of seemingly positive and negative energies, but the secret to interacting with life is to stop seeing things as positive and negative. Each situation is another reason to grow, another reason to go deeper inside ourselves. It's not a reason to bitch and complain and fight with other human beings. They're not the enemy. They're mostly unconscious people that struggle with their own lives. They should remind us to stay centered, to go deeper, to not let petty differences and tensions rip away the benefits of meditation class. My grandmother once said, "Everything passes." How true! Most of us can barely remember why we were angry with someone in the first place.

Life itself is the test, but life is also a succession of karmic developments that determine the evolution of each human being.

It's the guru reflecting both positive and negative qualities in each of us. Success at life depends on how happy we are at the moment of death. Success at life also depends on a conscious dialectic: Are life and death one and the same to us? Can we embrace them? Are we no longer frightened of the unknown? These are important questions but questions impossible to ask ourselves. Either we've evolved spiritually to the point that answers to these questions are simply part of our being, or we leave the world with karmic accumulation that needs to be completed in future lifetimes.

People often substitute meditation for a spiritual life. What's worse is they substitute living in communes, ashrams, or monasteries for a spiritual life. If they're macrobiotic or vegetarian; if they wear orange robes and turbans and smell of sandalwood incense; if they chant mantras, walk lightly, and speak in a quiet, holier-than-thou voice; if they play-act godliness most of the time, all of the above are just substitutions for spirituality. None of the above (including meditation) guarantees a spiritual life. Because someone attends meditation class Mondays and Wednesdays, because they sit there an hour each of those days and breathe heavy and absorb *shakti*, it doesn't mean they're going to get any closer to God. They're learning an exercise, that's all, and the exercise itself is not a spiritual life. It must be taken deep inside the practitioner. It must be worked with over long periods of time. It must be used to develop the chakra system. More important than anything else, it must be used to create a bridge between meditation class and the rest of life.

The meditation exercise is nothing more than a technique that helps us open to God. It's not a religion or a cult. It's not a fanatical order of sacred gibberish. It's nothing more than a craft used to build strong inner lives. The results of meditation practice become apparent while we have breakfast with our families, while we're on the job, in taxis, on the subway, at the end of the day when exhaustion sets in, at dinner, in front of the TV, and at parties and other gatherings. If our hearts are open, if the bagel or croissant tastes good, if there's sharing of love and respect, and if we can transcend petty urges to get upset, then we're learning to use meditation practice in daily life. We know we're becoming human when life's pressure increases and we can deal with it in a simple, quiet way. We know we're becoming more human when a New

173

York taxi driver almost gets us killed six times in ten minutes and we can say, without getting upset, "Hey, would you please drive a little slower or I'm going to get out of your cab?" We know we're getting more human when someone close to us gets sick and we deal with it consciously.

A student of mine in Brazil was held up at gunpoint by a thirteen-year-old kid. The kid threatened to kill her because she gave him a small amount of money, though she gave him all the money she had with her. She gently touched his face with her hand and asked him what's wrong. The kid broke into tears. He sat down and told her his life story. He even tried to give back the money. We become more human when we quietly touch the souls of other people. Even ragamuffin criminals have God inside them. We have to find it.

Years ago, I had a new student who practiced meditation at home. She once said to me, "I sit in my room for hours on end and burn incense, pray, meditate, and try to stay quiet, but the moment I leave my apartment for the streets, I freak out. What's the point of meditation?" I told her there's no point if she can't take meditation into her life. She's wasting her time. She's not building a foundation. She's not bridging the gap between the meditation room and the rest of her life. She's got to learn to live in the world and be free of the world at the same time. The ability to do this is the real test of a spiritual life.

CHAPTER FIFTEEN:

Healing

It's never disease that's the problem. It's the person who has the disease and the people around him. Longevity's not the solution to a boring life. It's better to live one minute consciously than 135 years like an idiot. Some trees live a thousand years, but so what? They're never anything but trees. People are similar. They're afraid to die. They cling to miserable, unhappy lives as if their miserable, unhappy life is worth living. But we all die from something. When we finally accept this, when we're no longer afraid of death and the unknown, the healing process begins, and we take a step toward becoming a whole person.

Disease and disharmony are almost synonymous. The body's field of balance is disrupted by blockages. Energy stops flowing. Acupuncturists stick needles into blocked meridians to release the flow of energy. They try to bring balance and harmony to the body, but the cause of disease stems from deep-seated tensions in a human being, tensions so strong they erode the cells and organs of the body. Years of wear and tear deplete the body's resistance. People get heart conditions, cancer, ulcers, and assorted diseases that can be healed. But, to be healed, first people have to change. They must quiet their minds and emotions, learn to master tension, and transform what's killing them into a life-giving force.

Most people with life-threatening illnesses don't want to live. They're tired of life's pressures. They want to be taken care of, to be loved, to be under the care of a nurse or physician. "Give me drugs, painkillers, a hospital bed, anything to escape the rigors of a tense world," they say. There's no more will to live. The disease

175

becomes the central focal point of their lives. In many cases, it's the only thing the sick live for.

Age and death are states of mind that can be overcome if we nurture our inner child. The will to live is deep within every person and meditation helps us to find it. It helps us to regenerate chakras that have atrophied; it helps us to heal ourselves of disharmonious bodies and minds.

Most people have life-threatening diseases before they think about healing themselves. They run to doctors, surgeons, and psychics, to anyone who can add a few years to their life. They rarely, if ever, heal themselves before they get sick. They rarely, if ever, use preventative measures to keep serious illness away.

Healers should never interfere with the death process. They should heal people who truly want to live, who are willing to change, who wish to master themselves and grow because of life-threatening diseases. Longevity doesn't mean anything. More importantly, how do we use time allotted to us? Why live a hundred and twenty years of boring existence? Wouldn't it be better to die, come back, and try again? The next lifetime might be a more creative one. We finally have to accept that death is as organic to the evolution of mankind as birth.

Of course, this brings up the question of suicide. Why not kill oneself if life's tedium, pain, and suffering are all too much? Suicide defies organic rhythms of nature. The same energy used in killing ourselves can also give us life. When we lose the will to live, in a sense, we've committed suicide. We've chosen death in life instead of the regeneration of life-affirming energies. We've chosen to repeat karmic situations in our next incarnation. Suicide resolves nothing. It prolongs the evolution of one's soul. We just have to come back and try it again. It's taken us nowhere.

How Tantra Heals

Healing is a transformative power that removes negative energy from our organs — a tantric practice that uses sexual energy to change illness into well-being. Sexual energy is the source of life in the world. It gives birth to new generations of people. It can also give birth to oneself.

If we draw energy from the chakra below the navel in a human being, through the sex chakra to the base of the spine, the sex chakra transforms *chi* into energy that activates kundalini. The conscious use of tantra changes lower elements of life into higher elements. Healers can transform disease into positive energy.

Many hands-on healers absorb the negative energy of disease into themselves when they try to channel spiritual energy to the sick person. The negative energy absorbed by the healer can cause them deep physical problems if they're not careful. It's not something to be done lightly.

The healer should drain all negative psychic tension from his or her own body after they've given hands-on treatment. They shouldn't absorb more than they can handle. They've got to learn to let the patient heal himself. Herein lies the secret of tantra. Instead of absorbing negative energy, the healer can draw it through the patient's sex chakra and transform it into a life-giving force that may not only save the ill person's life, but the healer's as well.

Sexual energy is a very powerful force that often scares people. There are so many taboos regarding sex that are dogmatically etched into the human mind. But the art of tantra teaches how to use sexual energy for meditational purposes, how to draw the energy to the base of the spine and activate the sleeping kundalini. Its force, when used properly, can transform a negative quantity into a regenerative, life-giving energy. It can heal people. Tantra can't be learned from books. It's a byproduct of deep meditation training, and it becomes part of our consciousness as we evolve closer to spiritual enlightenment. It's dangerous to apply tantric techniques learned by rote.

The healer has to surrender unconditionally to higher energy. He can't use healing to serve his egotistical purposes. The energy coming through him will not only harm the diseased person, but it will also do damage to the healer.

Most healers use their gift as a moneymaking device. They charge enormous fees to cure the sick. People come to them in desperate straits, people willing to pay anything to avoid the inevitable. Healing has become a rich man's game. Many play it who have no healing power. They have a little training in massage, colonics, and other forms of bodywork. They have medical and chiropractic degrees, and pharmaceutical licenses, but true healers

177

use their gift to serve God. They don't charge for the service. If they do charge, it's a very small fee. They also work with limited numbers of people, mostly serious spiritual students interested in transforming their illness into enlightenment.

We can never be completely healed. The human body will always be slightly out of balance. Only God is perfect. The rest of us have to suffer aches and pains. I don't care how healthy we are. When it comes to life-threatening diseases, meditation practice helps build a strong inner system that prevents the body from falling apart.

There are some basic truths we can't escape. Principal among them is that we all die from something. There's no escaping death's legerdemain. Perhaps the most important healing of all is to embrace death with joy, love, and deep gratitude. The alternative is to hang on to bedraggled threads of life, to fight a miserable battle against the inevitable. If we're not afraid to live, we're not going to be afraid to die, but unhappy people cling to every last breath. A happy person dies with nobility of soul. He's not afraid to embrace the unknown. He's lived his life to the fullest, and there's nothing to come back for. It's okay to go; it's okay to stay.

Pain and Suffering

Pain has frequency levels a person's will can transcend. It's a matter of detachment. If we center ourselves in the *hara* and keep the mind from attaching itself to the pain, the pain usually dissolves and goes away. Pain is too often fed by the mind. A small itch or ache grows into a monumental distraction because we focus the mind's attention on it. It's all we think about. If we detach ourselves from the itch or ache, if we stay centered in the *hara*, we starve the itch or ache, and it generally disappears. Wounds can also heal up in half the time.

Tolstoy wrote a short story called *The Death of Ivan Ilych*, a wonderful piece about a man who created the perfect life for himself. He had the perfect wife and child, the perfect job, the perfect house, the perfect china, and the perfect friends. He was a man proud of his accomplishments and who worked hard to maintain the status quo. There was only one problem. He had a pain in his gut. At first it was a small pain, but the pain grew to where he lost sight of everything but the pain. Doctors told him nothing could be done about the pain. Soon Ivan Ilych would die.

The pain consumed his mind and emotions and eventually the perfect world he had created for himself crumbled about him. His family's hypocrisy, the pettiness of coworkers, his house, horse, carriage, crystal, china, silver, and environment dissembled in front of his eyes. He was a victim of his own illusion. Naked and alone, having nothing to hang on to, in the last moments of his life, he found a path to God. His heart opened. The wise man became a fool who became a wise man again. He realized the transient nature of all things. His former perfection lacked spirit and happiness. He kowtowed to mediocrity. But moments before he died, his heart filled with joy and he made peace with God.

There's no price too costly to pay for spiritual enlightenment, but the pain experienced by most people over a sixty- or seventy-year lifespan is beyond comprehension. If being alive means we suffer, why not use suffering as an excuse to get to a higher place within ourselves? Why not let suffering be a reminder to open our hearts? Life costs anyway, so why not pay for it consciously?

Suffering should become an excuse to grow, a reason to open our hearts, a reminder of what the Earth is all about, a way to find compassion, forgiveness, love, and joy. It's the common denominator that binds people together from every part of the world. No one escapes its claws, but a few conscious people use suffering to get to God. The rest...? It's just pain and suffering linked to more pain and suffering. There's no exit from their own mad vision of life.

Stuart Perrin

CHAPTER SIXTEEN:

Ruminations on Surrender and the Spiritual Life

Using the Energy of Doubt

Years ago, I was in an automobile accident. The car went off the road and turned over. This was a terrible accident that could've hurt, if not killed the driver and me. While the car spun out of control and flipped over, I centered myself in the navel chakra. I had the sensation of being on an amusement park ride. Not one part of my body hit the car. At the same time, I put a protective shield around the driver, a psychic encasement to keep her from getting hurt. The car was totaled, but neither one of us was injured.

Every human being's life is transient. The time span between birth and death is short when compared to time's infinite nature, but we use time cheaply. We take it for granted. One day we're old, and life itself verges on the edge of termination. We no longer have the energy to effectively change ourselves. We're resigned to a death-in-life existence.

But age should bring wisdom. If nothing else, it brings perspective. Problems that afflict young people, like insecurity over career, marriage, the future, etc., vanish in age's overview of life's conundrums. If we've found the spiritual child in ourselves, if our inner lives are vital, happy, full of joy and love, though the body will have its share of aches and pains, age will do little or nothing to stop the evolution of higher consciousness.

Doubt, cynicism, and skepticism are three paths that lead

directly to a dead end. They're the mind's protective shield created from threads of fear that keep people from ever stepping into the unknown. They stop the creative process by reducing insight, imagination, instinct, and improvisation to structured mindsets that have most of the answers before questions are even asked. Doubt and skepticism siphon creative juice from people. They leave us empty, dead, and sterile, and they destroy the possibility of living life in the moment.

No one is ever completely free of doubt. It creeps into the thoughts of even the most spiritual people. Though the craft of meditation teaches us to transcend doubt, though we learn not to judge people's behavior, we often lose our centeredness. Our lack of balance gives the mind its opportunity to question everything it doesn't understand. We begin to doubt the very people and situations that gave us life in the first place.

As long as mind exists, there will be doubt, but mind can also draw the energy of doubt to the chakra below the navel. Mind can transform doubt into harmony and balance.

We master doubt by using will to deepen our inner lives, by humility, by an open heart, and trust in the world. The tension caused by doubt isolates people in their own brilliance. They know better than the rest of us. They don't trust what they see in karma's mirror. Their doubt and cynicism force life into an uneasy war that pits self-righteousness and opinion against mysterious forces that exist beyond logical, well-worked-out equations that satisfy mind.

Insecure people hide behind a veil of doubt. They're afraid of what they don't understand. All miracles, to them, have logical explanations. Their pragmatism reduces mystery to sterile interpretations of mind. They bury themselves in stratified layers of opinion and are too frightened to come out. They even have to understand God. Their brilliance inflicts a cynical skepticism on everyone they meet. Either we satisfy their vision of the world, or the wrath of ego descends on us. We're scorned, sneered at, made fun of, and called crazy mystics by doubting Thomases who hide behind a wall of fragile intelligence. But doubt has a positive aspect. Its discerning quality tells us when another human being is lying to us.

Listening to Fear

Fear's an emotional red light that warns us of danger. It's not an unhealthy state, unless the mind dwells on it, feeds it, and turns a simple signal into Godzilla. We have to listen to fear. It's telling us something's wrong, that there's danger or change, and that a situation's not what it's supposed to be. Fear demands centeredness; then, we're ready to deal with whatever danger lurks. If we lose ourselves to fear, if mind and emotion take over, a frenzied, frazzled, uncentered person walks directly into the arms of danger. We don't have a chance. If we listen to fear's message and center ourselves, we approach situations in a fearless way. We recognize the warning signal. It's telling us exactly what to do.

People fear death and the unknown. It's an intangible fear that lurks deep in the unconscious and sculpts our entire being. It forces us to look for security where there's none. It forces us to live lackluster and mediocre lives, to insulate ourselves against imaginary danger. "One day I'll be no more," we think. The very idea makes people hide in safe nooks and grottoes inside themselves. It's a senseless fear. We're going to die anyway. We might as well enjoy the lives we're given.

Detachment in the Center of Life

Detachment and apathy are often interpreted as one and the same thing. People think that, to be detached, they have to be apathetic. But apathy and detachment are very different issues. Apathetic people care little or nothing about life. They're usually lazy, unproductive, irresponsible souls that avoid pressure and commitment as if both were diseases. Detachment is another thing. We can't detach ourselves from what we haven't experienced. To be truly detached, we've got to be in the center of life. We have to be active, creative people unafraid to explore whatever avenues life opens to us.

A samurai is a good example of a warrior trained in the art of detachment. The greatest samurai sees both life and death as illusion, as partners in time, as reasons to stay centered in the *hara*. They've already fought the battle against self, perhaps the most difficult battle of all. They've liberated the mind from ego and thought from attachment to external things. They're poets, painters, calligraphers, gourmands, and assassins trained in the art of self-defense. War is secondary to them. Life and death are secondary to them. They've mastered the art of Zen and live their lives in the moment.

Meditation practice transforms the practitioner into a spiritual samurai. He need not become a hermit, or anchorite, or troglodyte, or anything but a spiritual warrior that lives in the marketplace. He loves life. At the same time, he learns to free himself of life's attachments by slowly but surely connecting his consciousness to God. He sees the thousand masks of higher energy. He enjoys them, he's open to them, he's grateful to them, he's not afraid of them, and he transforms all of them into spiritual enlightenment. He detaches his mind and emotions from life's eternal swamp, frees himself from himself and connects his spirit to God. Apathy is a whole other thing. Apathetic people don't give a damn about the marketplace. They're usually apathetic because they're too frightened to embrace life. They hide behind a shield of indifference. It keeps them from ever being spiritual warriors, from ever coming out of their carapace, from ever truly enjoying the wonders of God's spectacle.

I once heard a story about a monk who spent thirty years living in a cave. He was a holy man, an ascetic, religious man, and a practitioner of esoteric meditation who lived on roots and shrubs and grubs and berries. After thirty years of living in his cave, he decided to go to the marketplace to teach God's word. He made the long journey through forests and over pampas, across rivers and mountains, until he came to the gates of the city where he had a fight with the first beggar he met. He realized the marketplace had a great deal to teach him. Meditation and asceticism were only a small part of his spiritual education.

"The subtleties of life defy understanding," the monk thought. "It's not enough to meditate day and night. One must see God both in the cave and in the marketplace. A beggar wears the mask of God... a peddler shouts the words of God... a minstrel sings the verses of God. Meditation is not enough. I must let the marketplace teach me... I must learn to see God in every shadow and nuance of life. Then I'll be at peace here and in the cave."

The cave isn't the marketplace nor is the marketplace a cave.

God lives in both places. But knowledge of the cave doesn't mean we have knowledge of the marketplace. We have to live in and learn from both. It's impossible to detach ourselves from what we haven't experienced. Spiritual development needs to be tested by the rigors of the world. I'm often asked if I prefer the marketplace to the cave. Is that why I live in New York City?

It's hard to answer questions like that, but New York City works for me. It reminds me to stay centered, to stay balanced, and to work on myself every day. I like its bumps and grinds. I like the pressures and distractions. They force me to discipline myself.

It's so easy to navigate estuaries that go nowhere, but daily meditation practice keeps my boat on the river connected to higher energy in the universe. Instead of family, business, and an expensive life being excuses to stop meditation practice, they're a reminder to me that I need vast resources of spiritual energy to keep from drying up. Life's responsibilities take their toll. A car needs gas to operate; a refrigerator needs electricity; a boiler, oil; and a human being needs spiritual energy. Without it we turn into beef jerky. There's nothing left of us but an outer shell, a noisy brain, and fear of age and dying.

Most people have a "rent control" mentality. They look for the least expensive method of living life. They're afraid to give or receive unconditionally. They set up impenetrable fortresses around themselves, or, like moles, they hide in burrows fabricated from threads of fear and unhappiness. They're afraid to come out; they're afraid to take a chance. They're ruled by money (or the lack of money), power (or the lack thereof), and by a Pandora's box that seethes with anger, arrogance, fear, impotence, rage, and assorted other asp-like creatures that nest in the depths of human unconsciousness. They lack the wisdom and training of a spiritual samurai.

What is left is mind, relentless and predatory mind at war with itself and with anyone who enters its jurisdiction. The spiritual tanks remain empty. The heart has been siphoned of love, and human beings will go to any length (save deep spiritual work) to consciously or unconsciously refill their depleted inner lives.

The Fate of Passion

Passion, like most other desires, is a twofold path. It depends on where and how we direct it. When directed toward worldly goals, passion brings a return of both positive and negative results. When directed toward a spiritual life, it brings transcendental consciousness, a union of opposites, a oneness with God. If we direct passion toward money, it brings wealth and the spoils of wealth, but the road to wealth is littered with institutional juggernauts. We pay a large price for money. It revs up internal and external demons that leech off our energy. Every step on the path to wealth is replete with conflict. There are both positive and negative situations to be dealt with. The price is enormous, but wealth is a tangible, recognizable goal, one that brings power, comfort, financial security, and position. But wealth need not detract from a spiritual life, not if we detach ourselves from the glitter and illusion of success, and not if we recognize its transient nature.

They say, "It's easier for a camel to go through the eye of a needle than a rich man the doorway to heaven." There's much truth in this aphorism. The rich are so busy accumulating wealth and protecting their fortune from predators on every front that they forget about inner work. Money and power emit godlike auras of invincibility. They get people stoned. They open doors to the top of the material pyramid. The rich can buy whatever they like, but money, no matter how much of it's accumulated in a lifetime, has never opened the human heart for more than a few minutes at a time. When the passion for money fizzles, when the inner resources of the rich are drained, what's left is the shell of a person, a once-was that is no more, a person lost in memories of pinnacles climbed and dreams attained, a proud soul that lives in past events, a wounded spirit no longer able to function in life. Passion always fizzles, be it passion in relationships or passion for success and money. It drains us of our vital energy. We have to refuel the tank. Human beings can't run on empty. At some point, we have to internalize our passion. We have to use it to open chakras and connect with God. At some point, we have to replace what we spend; we have to keep from drying up.

Passion sculpts people's personae and inflates egos by extracting from life enormous success and by turning overly passionate people into caricatures of themselves. Success is necessary if we are to work out karma, but success at the expense of our humanity drains people of spirit. There's no reason to step over other people. The universe has enough abundance to provide for everyone. If we internalize our passion, if we use it to build strong inner lives, success and its spoils won't destroy us. If we learn to be happy, then we've managed to live the most successful life of all.

The Only Difference Is Consciousness

To cultivate love of God, one must start with basic life elements like breath, touch, sight, sound, and taste. People supplant the simple with the complex. They take for granted basics in their quest for money, power, and success, but each day's full of simple things. We eat, walk, talk, shit, sweat, drive, watch TV, and go to movies, shows, and picnics. There's no shortage of stuff to be grateful for. Rudi once asked me how he was different from other people. "What do I do every day?" he said about himself. "I sleep, eat, shit, shower, watch television, run a business, pay my bills, and I have pressures like everyone else. The only difference is consciousness. I'm grateful for each and every thing I do with my day." Rudi used basic elements of life to get closer to God.

Open-Heart Living

Life has a way of taking from us all the gifts it gives to us at birth. We're born innocent and pure and with open hearts. By the time we're five years old, most of these gifts have vanished. It's a rare human being who can spend a day with their heart center open. Therein lies ninety percent of the battle of meditation work.

It's impossible for the heart chakra to stay open if the other chakras are closed. It is like trying to grow a flower without a stem or roots. Given strong foundation, a quiet mind, and movement of energy through the sex chakra, the heart's essence will emit joy and love. It'll sparkle with gratitude; it'll speak the true language of God on Earth.

Tension keeps the heart closed. It surrounds a sea of love with crusty barnacles that cling tightly to a rusty vessel. The heart aches; it wants to open, but people forget to be grateful.

"At least an hour before every meditation class," I tell my students, "you should relax, open your hearts, and bring the highest level of self into the room. Why waste the class working against your own insanity? The mind should be quiet before we sit down to work. Then the class will be transcendental, not a forty-minute battle to quell inner demons."

The heart has tendencies to shrivel up and waste. It needs to be nurtured with love born out of self-worth, out of unconditional giving and receiving. Our youthful hearts are too often shredded by time's merciless lessons. There's no training.

Mostly, we need strength to love people who don't love themselves, people who leech off us, people who are too frightened to say thank you and mean it. We can never assume anything. As we get older, it's more difficult to keep the heart open. There's less energy, more defense mechanisms, less trust, and more to hide from. Our youth has been taken away from us. Without spiritual training, chakras atrophy, life passes, and our inner lives, once so young and fresh, waste like the body and mind waste, like most things about us that fall into ruin.

Real Power

Power's a subject difficult to define. It has many shapes and forms, and people sacrifice life and limb to lord it over other people. Real power emanates from the human heart. It manifests as love, compassion, humility, and forgiveness and makes us more human and less needy of protecting our minor league kingdoms from aggressive tactics employed by human sharks. No matter how vast our kingdom, it will fall into ruin and decay when subjected to the ravages of time.

Power makes us forget we're human, but love and compassion, so difficult to come by, so hard to sustain, remind us that we suffer, that other people suffer, that to give and receive unconditionally requires more strength than the strength required to run a multinational corporation. Both love and compassion touch the deepest parts of our humanity. If our hearts are open, there's no need to etch our egos into the world's consciousness. Less becomes better. There's more spirit in us and less opinion, more forgiveness and less dictatorial persona that lords it over less fortunate mortals that depend on us to earn a living. Only very strong people can live this way, people who bring higher consciousness to the world, who aren't afraid to love and be loved.

Will as a Tool

There are many doctrines in theology, like the will of God and the will of man, that confuse and discombobulate people. These are terms theologians debate ad infinitum. There never seem to be answers that satisfy everyone. I'm not the final authority on this subject, nor will I ever be. Theologians can drill holes in my ideas. They'll fight over the meaning of God's will and human will long after I'm dead and buried.

I take a common-sense approach. First, it's impossible to define God, not to my satisfaction or the satisfaction of anyone I've known through personal interaction, books, spiritual studies, or lectures. I wouldn't even try. Second, the struggle of human will versus higher will is an absurdity. Human beings cannot win the battle. The will of a man dies when a man dies. The will of higher energy bridges generation to generation. It's always there. When people vanish from Earth, higher energy continues to romp and play. This is all esoteric speculation. More importantly, the will of man is used every day to attain its ends. People are driven to power, success, and domination over other people. Rarely, if ever, do people internalize their wills and build strong inner lives that connect themselves to God. They're not ready to undertake deep meditation practice. They walk their individual paths like the pretentious naked ruler that heralds himself in the tale of the Emperor's new clothes, pompous, overbearing, blind to himself and others, he lived in a confused state that bordered egomania. His mind dominated every action. There was little or no consciousness of higher forces in the universe, and he lived like an absurd caricature in a Daumier cartoon.

Human will and divine will are part and parcel of the same puzzle. They're not in conflict with each other. The divine will awaits the evolution of the human will. Then it channels itself through people who've developed higher states of consciousness. But gifted people often assume they're enlightened. They play ego games in a dangerous arena, ego games that use magical powers to impress other people. They're not the servants of divine will. They're often servants of their own megalomania.

"So how does one separate a real spiritual teacher from a huckster?" people ask me all the time. A novice can't, but even a novice can take teachings from a teacher, use them to build his own life, and not worry about the guru's integrity. It's impossible to get hurt if one's sincere about spiritual growth. We can only get hurt if we play games. It's easy to play bodhisattva, to recognize other people's problems and advise them. Our own problems are hidden behind a mysterious cloud that separates us from higher creative energy.

No teacher is perfect. If we deify him, he's going to disappoint us. Only God is perfect. The rest of us have to grow every day. Why focus on a fictional guru created in our own minds? No teacher can live up to our version of godliness. We blind ourselves in spiritual illusion, and the guru is always out of reach.

Necessity determines how far we go with our spiritual practice. If our need is strong, if we master the art of internalizing will, if we discipline ourselves and work deeply at our daily meditation practice, doors will open on the path to enlightenment. But first our priorities must be clear. If we use will to break down blocks between ourselves and higher energy in the universe, then will becomes an essential tool in the building of a spiritual life. It dredges up lifetimes of inner garbage. It forces us to center ourselves, to discipline mind, emotion, and breath. It draws energy from chakra to chakra; and it gives us courage to fight an almost impossible battle against ourselves. That's conscious use of will.

Unfortunately, most of us externalize will. We use it to advance ourselves no matter what the cost to others. Then will has only one purpose, and that is power. Once it tastes power, it continues to plunder the hearts of people as it moves on its gluttonous way.

Willpower is a sacred gift and, when used consciously, it demands that we work on ourselves. It gives us the strength to overcome the impossible. If used consciously, will becomes another weapon that battles inner resistance. It sets priorities and then works to attain them. When we connect the power of will with our need to be spiritually enlightened, we've won a very important battle. It's a major step in linking our consciousness with transcendental energy.

Death and Samadhi

People who are on the brink of death open easily to God. They no longer have the strength to resist the inevitable. Suffering breaks down resistance to spirit; suffering voids rational answers to irrational problems. Terminally ill people are forced to surrender; they're forced to confront their own mortality.

My father died a slow, painful death, a feverish death that burned resistance from the very core of his being. In the last hours of his life, he became my first spiritual teacher. His eyes were clear, his words simple and wise, and the hospital room was full of light, energy, and a sense of peace I'd never experienced before. "This happens to most people before they die," a nurse said to me. I was sixteen years old at the time. Why did he have to wait forty-nine years to experience such deep peace? I thought. Why didn't he live his life that way? His death transformed my consciousness, and I set out on the spiritual path.

Though most people succumb to God just before death, their act of surrender is simply preparation for the bardo realm between this incarnation and the next. It's not conscious work to attain spiritual enlightenment.

Deep meditation practice prepares us for *samadhi*, a state of grace in which the soul of a human being is married to the universal soul. This union enables the soul to enter realms outside of time and space. These realms transcend astral planes, bardo consciousness, gods, goddesses, angels, seraphim, devas--anything the human mind can understand. The soul is liberated from rounds of karma. It no longer has to return to Earth's program of continuous education.

Samadhi is the byproduct of a lifetime of spiritual practice. It doesn't just happen because we embrace death. To attain *samadhi*, we have to master the subtle planes that exist between the Earth and the cosmos. We have to experience our own nothingness. We have to surrender everything to higher energy in the universe.

Believing the Dream

We attach ourselves to cults and causes and institutionalized religions, to gurus and swamis and priests and rabbis, to the idea of God and to preconceived notions on how to live a spiritual life—most of which exists in our own minds. We're not who we think we are, nor who we pretend to be.

Rarely, if ever, do we reach into the vast wellspring of inner consciousness. The mind forbids it. The mind directs consciousness into the illusion of spirituality. We assuage deep inner needs by accepting saccharine answers to difficult questions. It's easy to attach ourselves to quasi-spiritual communities. We're lonely and frightened, in need of a boyfriend or girlfriend, desperate to escape life's pressures, and we substitute dogma for deep spiritual work.

We can't enjoy life if we're attached to it. Our emotional and mental static interferes with clear views of reality. Every situation drains us of energy. But life's spectacle is what it is, an ever-changing kaleidoscope of dreamlike events that reflect the complex nature of human beings. When we open to it, learn from it, and just let it be, life guides us on the path to spiritual enlightenment.

Self-Confidence

People always have opinions about what's right or wrong for us, opinions based on preconceptions that dangle in their own minds. It's impossible to convince everyone that what we do is beneficial. Though meditation practice is precious to the practitioner, there will always be someone who finds fault with it. Detractors test our conviction. We have to look in karma's mirror everyday and take note of changes in our lives. Results are all that matters.

People's opinions shift and change like the weather, but a connection with higher energy, a more human approach to one's life, a clear path through a dense forest, should deepen the conviction that spiritual practice works. It doesn't matter what other people say. It takes guts to step into uncharted worlds. When we tap inner storehouses of creative treasure, when our lives are rich and full and remind us how transient and illusive are opinions of men, when we listen carefully to our inner voice and we remember its precious sound made more precious by spiritual awareness, why should detractors make a difference? Why forget how difficult it is to gain a foothold in realms of higher consciousness? Why throw it away because of someone else's opinion? We have to respect other people's lives and not feel compelled to make them do what we do. They've made their choices; so have we. It's best to leave them alone, to let them be, to let them live their lives and struggle with their problems without us guiding them through a labyrinthine network of our own preconceptions. They want love from us, not advice. Advice, no matter how profound or pointed, usually chases people away.

The opinions of people should not taint our spiritual perspective. If I made a list of comments and slurs made about my personal life and meditation practice by students, relatives of students and ex-students, the gossip alone would make the *National Enquirer* look like a children's book. Does it really matter? Why should it? I've seen what spiritual work has done for my life. I've seen it change me over the last thirty-five years. What does it matter what people say? It's their problem, not mine. I just do my work everyday. The rest drifts into the great yawn of time.

It's difficult enough to sustain my inner work without getting involved in other people's dramas. If they don't understand what I do, they should come and ask. I'd be happy to tell them. Putting other people down is an easy way to satisfy ego. It's an easy way to relieve the threat of someone who lives a more creative life than we do.

Even so, there are a thousand reasons not to do spiritual work, yet, as I see it, everything in life should be a reminder to work deeper in myself. It's easy to say, "I have a headache, a cold, a date, a party, a meeting, too many problems, no problems at all" Any excuse will do. We can also say, "Problems are God's way of telling me to do something about myself. Why complain about them? No matter what I do, they're not going to go away." All of recorded history is about problems. It's stupid to think we're going to be spared them, but we live with "Why me?" complexes. The energy wasted complaining about problems could be just as well used to build strong inner lives.

Deep meditation practice is so precious it's impossible to sell it to anyone else, but religious fanatics often work hard to convert others to their religions. It's a foolish game played by insecure people that try to convince other insecure people their chosen path is the only righteous one. The thought of converting anyone to kundalini yoga is laughable. People have to come to it on their own. When they're ready, the master will be there.

Spiritual work takes place in the silence of our own heart. We're well aware of the obstacles between ourselves and higher energy. It's difficult to face them, so we hide in insulated corners of ourselves and peek out at a scary world. Once we taste the nectar of spiritual energy, once we're awakened to growth possibilities in meditation practice, there's nothing to gossip about, nothing to be afraid of, and nothing but a well of deep inner silence to draw sustenance from, to be grateful for, to use every day in our lives. Why talk about it and dilute the experience?

What works for us will not necessarily work for our friends, relatives, and acquaintances. To convince them to practice meditation is a fool's ploy. Most people are not ready. It's better to talk about baseball, basketball, the cost of real estate, and the whims of the stock market. At least there's common ground for communication. If you pontificate on kundalini yoga, your mother, father, or best friend might think you're a madman or an idiot. It's a quick way to estrange yourself from people close to you. It's better to have patience. If they comment on how well you look, it's okay to tell them you practice meditation, but give them the phone number of your teacher and say, "If you're interested, he can explain it much better than I." Why lecture them on the esoteric nature of chakras and their link between Earth and heaven? They probably won't understand anyway. It's like first-term psychology students analyzing everyone they meet. It could be dangerous.

Even a Spring Day Has a Soul

Energy manifests on Earth in many different ways, from the densest stone to plants, animals, water, air, and light. Energy takes on infinite shapes, sizes, and forms. All are part of the design of life.

Years ago, I met an old lady who worked as curator and manager of the Jacques Marchais Museum of Tibetan Art in Staten

Island. We became friendly. She had asked me if I wanted to make use of the museum's library. "There are many books on the occult," she said when I first met her. Then one day, in the museum's garden, she said something to me I've never forgotten. "Everyone's afraid of reincarnation. They're afraid they'll come back as a toad or worm or jellyfish or whatever. Me, I don't care. I'd just like to come back to Earth like a spring day," she said. It made me think that even a "spring day" has a soul. What a short, wonderful, and exquisite visit to Earth. I never saw her again, but her words have always stayed with me.

God's spectacle on Earth includes the ant, toad, shrub, oak, lion, weasel, rose bush, and hundreds of millions of other forms life takes. It's all part of evolution. The soul moves through countless forms until it becomes conscious of higher energy, until it evolves through the human form and becomes one with God. All of creation is one with God, but the soul's work on Earth is to become conscious of the design of the universe, to attain enlightenment, to free itself of manifestation, and to merge with realms outside of time and space.

We Struggle with Everything

A student once asked me why we struggle with angels if angels are supposedly good for us. "We struggle with everything," I said by way of answer, "both good and bad, and that includes angels." We struggle to eat properly, to stop drinking alcohol, to stop smoking, to clean up polluted cities, to make money, to have relationships. Almost everything in life precipitates struggle. So we struggle with angels, too, even if they try to get us to open to God; even if they try to guide us on the cosmic ladder; even if they bring lightness, simplicity, joy, color, and astral energy; but we still fight with them. Angels slay ignorance, neurosis, and unhappiness and quell demons inside us, but we continue to resist them. In fact, we resist anything beneficial to our spiritual growth.

Inner Eyes and Ears

From the moment of birth, parents inculcate preconceived patterns of behavior. We can't blame them. They just don't know any better. Most people are trained to see with their physical eyes, but many creative types see with a mystical inner eye. They look in on a world of angels. They peruse, at will, the "magical mystery show" on the astral plane of consciousness. They listen with an inner ear to the *Om* sound, to voices of spirit guides, to the sound of energy that manifests at the beginnings of time.

Some people are born with this oddball gift, and others get it through meditation practice. The latter has to be retrained. Initially, they're taught by parents and schoolteachers to see and hear only concrete sights and sounds. Rarely, if ever, do parents mention inner eyes and inner ears. Rarely, if ever, do we hear parents speak about angels. It's forbidden ground, mysterious terrain, yet it is the next stage in the evolutionary process of a human being.

It's hard for people to accept a spiritual life. It's hard for us to believe union with higher energy is possible. We relegate yogic practice to ascetic *sadhus* that live on the banks of the Ganges. "Imagine," I've heard people say, "a spiritual life in Manhattan. What tomfoolery! What an absurd notion! I'm too busy just try-ing to pay rent."

Spirit is lost in the clamor of daily events. We don't hear with an inner ear nor do we see with the third eye. We witness a no-nonsense world full of shapes, forms, and pressurized situ-ations. The creative part of us has died an early death. We're left with a chorus of voices screaming, "Be this! Be that! Work at a job you hate! Build a career you hate! Money and power are the only measures of success in life!" But the truth of the matter is very different. Happiness is the only measure of success in life. All the rest is wisdom proposed by spiritually deaf, dumb, and blind people.

Beauty in the Eyes

It's wonderful to see a spiritual life manifest in the eyes of people I love. A sparkle emanates directly from their hearts. A clear radiance transforms dull-eyed lost souls into happy human beings. Chaos and confusion disappear. Countenances change. People once miserable and unhappy, people with flaking skin and tired eyes, hunched people and bent people, people that suffer from all manner of diseases, suddenly become beautiful. It's a beauty no fashion magazine can match, a beauty rooted in the soul and centered in the human heart. It doesn't require cosmetics and perfumes. No stylist can recreate love that mysteriously makes its presence known, love that flows from deep recesses in the human soul. Love, joy, and happiness—Beauty has a deeper essence than fashion surreptitiously brainwashing millions of people. It hides behind layer upon layer of tension and won't come out until people shed superficial disguises and find within themselves reasons to be happy. No human being should be denied this. We're all born here to have wonderful lives, but people torture themselves for little or no reason.

Life is very precious. It's the one gift given to all of us. Why throw it away on unresolved problems? Why deny ourselves the right to be happy? I've been asked many times to define enlightenment. I usually chuckle for a few seconds, then say, "Enlightenment is being happy, living in the moment, being conscious of God's spectacle on Earth." If people want more exotic answers, they'll have to get them from someone else. It's like the parable written by the Sufi poet Rumi about a stork standing in a lake complaining it's dying of thirst.

There's abundance in life, yet we're trapped in dark little prisons we create for ourselves, prisons fabricated from mind, emotion, and matter, prisons built directly at the heart of spiritual abundance. We see what we want to see, hear what we want to hear, and then forge lonely paths through magical kingdoms full of spiritual treasure. Instead of drinking from the pond, we complain. Instead of filling ourselves with God's wonder, we latch on to neurotic solutions to simple problems. Instead of being grateful for life's precious gift, we use it cheaply.

We sleepwalk through a spiritual wonderland. The moment we wake up, less becomes more, a leaf becomes as much a treasure as a precious stone, and the air we breathe becomes sacred. We're no longer lost in chaotic mind sets that force us to live at the edge of oblivion. Whatever we need to have a spiritual life is given to us. It's never farther away than the water at the feet of Rumi's stork.

I often look into the eyes of people that walk past me on the street and see dank, almost empty hallways with ten-watt light bulbs that shine in the distance — frenzied, neurotic activity that covers up vacant stares. I wonder how long it takes them to realize little Alice is so close to Wonderland. All she needs to do is climb down the well. But how do we tell people the well is inside them? How do we guide them to treasures so readily available? It can't be done. They have to be ready to listen. It's like water flowing past a rock. Nothing gets absorbed. Wisdom and stupidity are the same thing to people that wallow in their own lack of consciousness. A twenty-carat clear diamond is just another rock.

Spiritual energy is the key to conscious living, but most people substitute junk food spirituality for a healthy diet—the more superficial, the better. Why probe the depths of the unconscious if we can slip by without making an effort? That's how new-age hucksters can prey on lazy spiritual seekers. They sell heaven in a crystal, healing in soft voices, chakra development in computer programs, God in a stick of incense, and *shakti* bottled to go. It's like W C. Fields selling sugar water as medicine in an Old West sideshow. People buy into anything that'll give them a kick. New-age spirituality is prime time for hustlers that sell cosmic doodads.

Nothing replaces simple, honest meditation practice. It brings the best results. When the mind and breath are taken deep within us, they open the chakra system and connect our consciousness to higher energy in the universe. The tools of spirituality give us self-reliance and independence. More importantly, they open the heart chakra and allow the radiance of cosmic energy to sparkle in our eyes.

Floating on Muddy Water

Spiritual Energy is the most powerful force in the universe. In the Bhagavad-Gita, when Krishna reveals himself to Arjuna, he's not a wimpy clown that lifts five-pound weights. He's like a thousand suns that suddenly appear in the sky. Everything that's ever lived from the beginning of time rushes headlong into his fire. Meditation practice prepares us to see that vision. It creates the perfect democracy, not caring about race and religion, regional or national borders. Meditation prepares practitioners to witness the spectacle of higher energy in the universe by strengthening their inner lives. It is a process of awareness that unfolds over long periods of time.

We have to be strong to stand in front of God. We need balance, foundation, clarity, and an open heart, and, above everything else, we need to free ourselves of karmic restrictions so we're no longer caught up with the tensions of life. They no longer separate us from Krishna's divine song.

It's a long voyage to Krishna's big toe. When we climb aboard the spiritual ship, we commit ourselves to a life of surrender. We commit ourselves to searching for the most difficult treasure of all: spiritual enlightenment, oneness with God, the spectacle of creation that manifests around us.

Rudi used to say, "If you want to have an extraordinary life, you have to be willing to make an extraordinary effort."

Most evolved spiritual teachers weren't born from lotus flowers. Rudi was born in the slums of Brooklyn. He fought his way out of lower middle-class America to spiritual enlightenment. He taught a form of survival yoga based on street smarts and common sense. There was room on his table for bagels, lox, cream cheese, roast beef, pecan pie, astral traveling, bardo work, business, and total surrender to higher energy in the universe. I once heard him say, "The symbol for Buddhism is the lotus flower. Lotus flowers grow out of mud. Human beings also grow out of mud. They, too, have to learn to float on muddy water."

A Grounding In the Basics

Meditation practice teaches us to return to basics. Great cosmic visions and kundalini experiences are important, but without basic levels of inner work, out-of-body experience, astral travel, and the rest of the spiritual pizazz, can make us cut the moorings from the wharf and our cozy little spiritual ship will drift out to sea. They're too powerful. They can drive a person crazy. We need to be well-rooted on Earth; we need to be centered in the navel chakra; we need to make conscious use of mind and breath and never forget our humanity.

Musicians practice basics all the time. So do athletes and plumbers, architects and engineers. The best of them never forget basic knowledge when they apply their craft. Every tree and plant has roots, and most animals have nests or lairs to return to. We're no different. We can't get swept away in a cosmic rush. There are simple elements that make a spiritual life possible. We can neither forget them nor take them for granted.

Ordinary life requires grounding in basics. For instance, family is basic. Jobs, businesses, and daily responsibilities are basic. We can't forget about them. No matter how hard we try, there's no way we can escape our parents. No matter where we run, we take them with us. It's best to heal old wounds by loving our parents, by being grateful to them. No matter what they did to us in the past, they still gave birth to us. They're the channel we took to enter the world. To hate our parents is to hate ourselves; it is to wish we were never born. People close to us always push our buttons. Sometimes it seems like that's their function. They remind us how fragile we are and how easily we fall prey to emotions. We can't hide from them. For instance, most mothers are masters at finding faults no matter how well we conceal them. They're like Sherlock Holmes and Hercule Poirot on a case. Nothing escapes their eagle eyes. Either we're strong enough to withstand the barrage of criticism, or we run from it like a rabbit that flees hunters.

Most of our parents have no spiritual training, but they have opinions like the rest of the world. They, too, like you and me, struggle with their own lives. Most of our parents have yet to learn to love themselves, but whether they love us or not is secondary to our need to love them and forgive them their sins. They gave birth to us. They're a necessary force in the evolution of our karma.

If we try to escape our karma, we get crazy. We begin to hate ourselves and cripple any real potential for a creative life. Inner strength developed by deep meditation practice cuts through self-hatred and teaches us to love ourselves. It's not ego love; nor self-involvement nor megalomania; but simple love; conscious love; the ability to sustain happiness through difficult situations; the ability to empathize with parents, children, spouses, relatives, and friends that struggle to make ends meet in their own lives. They, too, are trying to make sense out of a senseless world. They, too, blow it, just as we blow it, just as the whole world blows it most of the time.

The greatest teachers speak about forgiveness, a trait important to learn for no other reason than it relieves us of resentment and anger. It allows us to move on. It makes room for other people to be in our lives. We forgive them things they've done to us, or, worse yet, things we think they've done to us. Resentment is often a byproduct of our neurotic view of life, a view most people can't align themselves with, their minds being serious culprits in the forgiveness wars. Once the mind is quiet and the heart open, it's possible to go past indiscretions and petty annoyances and live our lives like human beings.

This is all basic, but we forget the basics. There's so much pressure and tension in life that it takes less than a split second for us to forget we've forgiven someone and to resent their existence. We attracted a victim on whom it's possible to vent repressed anger and deep-seated insecurity. We're armed with pointed verbal abuse and it's aimed at a loved one or a friend. We say things to them we wouldn't say to an enemy.

Forgiveness is forgotten until our anger exhausts itself. Then, in the calm of the moment, we feel sorry for what we said. We cry and ask forgiveness and make promises almost impossible to keep. It's a new round, a second chance, and another opportunity to learn that love is a better way of communicating than anger.

Spiritual talk is absurd if the fabric of our humanity is rent with insecurity and tension, if we forget forgiveness is an ongoing state of letting go. People we love shouldn't be victims of our anger. Their limitations should remind us to have more compassion, more love, and more understanding of how difficult it is for anyone to get through the day. We have to surrender our own insecurity and let people live around us. They're always going to make mistakes. They're always going to do things we don't like. If we support people through difficulties instead of fighting with them, we've taken a major step towards becoming human. The basics are in place. When we've mastered forgiveness and compassion, a spiritual life is possible.

Our view of reality forces us to look at life "through a glass darkly." No one and nothing fits into our lens. It's like putting a square peg in a round hole. Once we surrender "our reality," once we let go of self-righteous blather, another reality sets in, one replete with surrender, love, forgiveness, and a deeper sense of our purpose on Earth.

Inherent Goodness

There's basic goodness in every human being. Finding it is often not easy work, but beneath a crusty shell of negativity, there's a child in all of us that wants to be held and loved and listened to. It takes a big-hearted person to find that child, to peel away layer upon layer of defense and extract sweetness and joy and humanity in another person.

People are frightened of being loved. It means they have to expose themselves. It's easier to let the crust thicken than expose large, gaping, painful, loveless voids. It is easier to flounder around in self-delusion than succumb to real affection.

There's inherent goodness in every person, but it's well guarded by persona and hidden beneath stratified layers of insecurity and tension. The child in us plays in an Eden-like nursery off-limits to the well-intentioned but restricted mindset of its adult caretaker. The child in us trusts life, God, goodness in the world, simplicity, and potential for spiritual growth. It's attacked every day by armies of cynicism, but, by hook or crook, it survives an unbelieving world and continues to search for God. When people discover their inner child, usually after years of deep spiritual work and conviction, the inner child changes them. They enter its Eden-like nursery. There, they nurture themselves on love, goodness, innocence, and trust. There, they learn to speak God's language on Earth.

Stay Tuned for More Stuff

We fret and worry about what's next on life's agenda. Each day is linked to the next day by a contiguous chain of small and large events. Years ago on TV, a program called "The Gong Show" featured bad to semi-bad amateurs judged for talent by a panel of show-business celebrities. Before every intermission, the master of ceremonies would stand center stage, raise his arms in the air, and say, "Stay tuned for more stuff." He made me laugh. His "stuff" reminded me of life. What's next? What's on the agenda? How much more absurd can it get? What ludicrous conundrum will karma send? I often wished I could "gong" one experience after the other.

The more I grow spiritually in my life, the less seriously I take karma's conundrums. No riddle is worth the angst. I'd rather befriend the child that lives in my heart. It knows more about life than I do. The more childlike we become, the less we worry about life's pressure. We're not afraid to let life teach us about love and joy. The child in me always says, "I don't know about right and wrong. You'll have to go somewhere else to learn that. But you and I can dance before God. Is there anything more important than that?" What can I answer? The child also says, "Whether you're right or wrong amounts to nothing. Both are traps. Both have to be surrendered if you want to get closer to God. So dance and enjoy yourself because the music doesn't stop, and 'stuff' keeps coming and you and I will shake, rattle, and roll our way to the center of God's heart."

Unconditional Lovemaking

There's little or nothing given and received on Earth unconditionally. The word itself scares people. Life is a tit-for-tat game played by big and little power brokers, all of them looking for the edge. There's nothing wrong with this, as long as we're conscious of how to play the game, as long as we know how to weave the tapestry.

There's much lip-service gratitude in life from people who talk a good game, who readily say thank you, but rarely, if ever, show gratitude in their daily actions. They don't know how to give or receive. They're afraid of being vulnerable. They've paralyzed themselves in an ongoing stream of superficial response. Often these people are very sweet, but it's a saccharine sweetness, a holier-than-thou attitude, a sweetness without depth, a sweetness that disappears when there's a little pressure, a sweetness that sugarcoats an inability to give. These people are usually takers. They leech on to spiritual practice and unabashedly feed themselves without contributing an iota of food to the table. They usually fall away from a situation when pressure is put on them to contribute something real.

Spiritual work teaches unconditional surrender. That doesn't mean we let every weasel in the world walk over us. It means we give from the center of our hearts. We take joy in giving and expect nothing in return. We give because we're grateful to life. The alternative's a tit-for-tat power broker's game with mankind and God, a form of giving that doesn't open doors to higher consciousness. Most people play tit-for-tat. There's no reason to be angry or resentful towards them; just play them tit-for-tat with an open heart. Life's a game, anyway. We can play with our inner child, with spiritual power brokers, or with tit-for-tatters. There's no reason why any of the above should force us to close our hearts.

To forgive someone doesn't mean we have to interact with them the rest of our lives. We simply cleanse ourselves of anger, vengeance, and other heavy baggage we carry with us no matter where we go. If the forgiven is capable of forgiving, then both parties can walk common ground, but usually that's not the case. People are not mature enough to let go of grudges. We must forgive them their indiscretions because we have to move on in our own lives. It's enough that we have to carry our own baggage. Why carry someone else's as well?

Love is similar. It's easy to say I love you, but love, in a deeper sense, has little or nothing to do with what comes out of our mouths. "I love you" becomes "I hate you" as emotional winds shift. Love isn't a fleeting thing. It's not whirlwind emotions that grip us by the sex. It's a state of unconditional surrender in which patience, compassion, and forgiveness hold court. We don't possess the people we love, nor do they possess us. They reflect the joy that's in our own hearts. No one need say a word. It could be a simple glance, a touch, a gift, an offering of tea and cake and fruit.

Unconditional love finds its rightful place in gifts we give. The cake, tea, and fruit taste better. They're not replete with our tension. We've offered the deepest part of ourselves to a person who's grateful for the offering. The act of lovemaking is a form of meditation in which we give and receive energy so strong it transforms our tension into spirituality. Unconditional lovemaking takes place in the human heart. It allows us to experience the fullness of our own humanity.

Not Rejection, but Surrender

It's difficult to understand the meaning of surrender. It's not just a word; it's a state of openness that carries us from moment to moment in life. It allows us to let go of attachments and evolve to higher states of consciousness. Rudi's last words were, "a deeper sense of surrender." Words spoken from his heart, they acknowledged his own nothingness and his need to be one with God. He let go of life's attachments and accepted spiritual work as the highest level of activity on Earth. It made the pain of living bearable. He used it to attain deeper states of inner awareness and a sense of surrender to God. It gave him true independence and forced him to recognize his dependence on and connection to every living thing. "It's not rejection," he said more than once. "It's surrender."

Rejection is the act of an immature person. Surrender is the act of a human being who wants to be spiritually enlightened. We can't surrender what we haven't experienced, but we can reject anything and everything not to our liking. Rejection's an easy cop-out. The mind says yes or no according to preconceived tastes. We often reject the exact thing that'll make us grow. Conscious choice is another matter. We say yes or no depending on whether or not a situation will help develop more creativity. Many actors reject difficult parts. The great actors have a need to be tested. They want to play Hamlet and Lear and Macbeth. The test of Shakespeare deepens their acting craft. If they don't fully succeed in realizing the part, so what? Success is more subtle than a critic's pen.

Why reject anything until we've discovered its inherent possibilities, until we've seen whether or not it's necessary to our evolution? We should let go of dead weight, of things that no longer test our creativity, of the past and all its ghosts. But we can't be free of anything until we've experienced it. This is a difficult concept to understand. If we're rigid, dogmatic, or conceptual, if we follow the mind's dictates, then there's no room in our lives for experimentation. We're afraid to take a chance.

I loved Rudi's sense of disciplined abandon. It took him to the edge of life. He never hid behind fear or covered up his vulnerability. After years of meditation practice, surrender became organic to his nature. He followed its path to enlightenment.

What Mind Can — and Can't — Do

Meditation practice disintegrates ego into ash, and from ash a phoenix bird rises into the cosmos and becomes one with higher creative energy. Ash symbolizes death, and the phoenix is a symbol of rebirth. Both are necessary to spiritual evolution.

The mind limits consciousness to what it understands. It creates duality from oneness and fractures a harmonious universe by analyzing polar opposites and convincing us they're whole. Mind creates conflict where there is none. We don't need its thinking apparatus to be conscious. We need its pure energy focused in the foundation of our being, energy like a scalpel that cuts away deep inner obstacles. Facts clutter our brain, but clear light, peace, and harmony—a quiet mind and balance—these states of awareness bring consciousness. They allow knowledge and wisdom to flow through us. They allow us to be channels for higher energy in the universe.

It's absurd to think we can fit infinite energy into the mind's limited spectrum, but people try anyway. They're locked into rational perceptions of an irrational world. The inner boundaries crack. There's too much pressure, too much knowledge, too many facts, and none of it relieves tension that surrounds the human heart. The perimeters of mind are miniscule when compared to the universal soul. It's like a piece of sand in the desert. The slightest wind shifts its position. It can't quite figure out where to land, so it stays adrift.

The mind has its function, but as a rational, thinking entity, it interferes with wisdom's true nature; it limits us to what it understands. The universal soul has no limitation, and the mind, as vast and acute as it can sometimes be, is simply an energy force that works within the vast spectrum of consciousness.

Silence

Beneath the noise of the streets the voices of people, the chit-chat of the mind, the subtle sounds of music, nature, and every human heartbeat, there's silence so profound it consumes the universe. Most human beings have cut their connection with silence. They don't even know where to look for it. They sail the

Earth on drunken boats that barely touch a windless sea. They don't know how to navigate or map a journey to the center of silence. They look everywhere, but everywhere is nowhere on a vast and endless ocean of water.

The silence is deep inside us. It waits patiently for us to uncover its secrets. We're always alone until we find its voice. It doesn't matter if we're surrounded by thousands of people. Loneliness has nothing to do with friends and acquaintances. It has to do with one's own state of inner peace. If we connect with silence, we'll never lack for life's boundless spiritual treasures. All thought, emotion, and other noise cover up deep hunger in human beings for silence's sublime state of grace that is connected to the wisdom of God. Why spend day and night living in a cordon of fear? Silence shows us impermanence, mutability, transience, a world replete with illusion, a dreamworld, and a vast inner consciousness that connects our soul with infinite energy in the universe.

It's our work to find silence, not the work of silence to find us. We have to make a conscious effort to dredge up and remove obstacles to silence, to hack our way through inner terrain, to need spiritual enlightenment more than any other goal on Earth.

People think that meditation is practiced by wimps and flakes and hippies and dippies and all manner of space cadets that try to avoid responsibility in life. But meditation weeds them all out. Its bottom line shows serious students with serious needs how to do whatever it takes to have a spiritual life. Meditation requires responsibility, not avoidance of responsibility and drifting in a void. It's not for flakes. They always find excuses to drift away. Meditation is for serious students who wish to stay in touch with silence. If silence requires responsibility, they don't turn their backs on silence and avoid work. They don't run from life's social fabric. They can live in the world and outside the world at exactly the same time.

Why Fiddle-Faddle with God?

Meditation is too difficult a practice for people to do without deep inner commitment. For someone to sit still forty-five minutes a day, seven days a week, and breathe into heart and navel without a fundamental need to grow spiritually, for someone to go through the motions of deep meditation without believing in what they're doing, that someone is either a very lonely person or a madman. Deep meditation isn't for everyone. I've never seen armies of people practicing it. Meditation itself culls the crowd. It eliminates people who aren't ready. The work is too hard.

It's easy to trick ourselves into believing life's thin veneer of jocularity and comfort will last, but time wears down even the most gilded of thrones. Age comes, sickness comes, and the veneer peels up in the weather. Nothing's left but empty caskets and empty dreams. Meditation does little or nothing to help dead souls. Time wears thin the appearance of bloated egos, leaving cracked images of self. Then people desperately seek help. They even listen to the advice of meditation instructors, gurus, and religious leaders, people they've spent most of their lives laughing at. But desperation won't take us far on the spiritual path. It's the wrong vehicle. It makes us grasp at tidbits of teaching and insight. There has to be a deeper need, a *spiritual* need. Without the latter, it's form without essence, craft without substance, and we paddle our boat on an empty lake.

There's little or no point in practicing meditation without a deep need to grow and change. Why fiddle-faddle around with God? It'll take you nowhere. It's easy to fool other people, but deep inside, every human being knows whether or not they're full of shit. The rest of humanity finds out later. So why spend forty-five minutes breathing heavy and gloating in strong spiritual energy if you refuse to take that energy to a place in yourself connected to higher consciousness? It's a waste of everyone's time. It might assuage little guilt feelings. "At least I'm doing something about myself," people say. "I'm attending meditation class. I'm learning to grow." But the sounds of those little pats on the back fade quickly. The moment that people hit resistance, they find a multitude of excuses to be out the door.

The moment we develop a belief system and dogmatically defend principles we think are right, we've got to surrender our beliefs and become open to new levels of creativity. Belief systems crystallize us in minor-league dictatorial regimes. It's better to listen to other people's ideas than force them to follow our own. It's better to compromise our ideals than fight wars to protect them. Nobody has a monopoly on rightness.

More people have been killed in the name of religion than any other institution known to mankind. They're blinded by dogma created for man by men to trap men in fanatical orders of frenzied zealots who have a beeline to the big toe of God. The rest of us are condemned to hell. We were born wrong. Conceived in an apostate's belly, we're condemned to burn through all eternity in Lucifer's barn fire. We never had a chance to make up for our parents' night of reckless lovemaking. It is futile to complain. Zealots don't listen, anyway. It's better to learn from them what not to do. It's better to transcend rightness, to find a less dictatorial path to God, to be grateful for eternal perdition if it relieves us of having to spend time with fanatical fringe freaks who preach the doom of innocent babes.

The Covenant with the Mother

Kundalini energy rises up the spine to the crown chakra, accumulates there, forms what's known as the Buddha's bump, then opens the crown and allows the soul force of a human being to move into the cosmos and merge with God. It's the chariot we ride to the genesis of time, to the moment in which all things come into being.

When meditation practitioners have evolved to where they're ready to embrace the Mother Goddess––call her Kali, Shekinah, the Virgin Mary, or Uma, it doesn't matter––the Mother Goddess responsible for immaculate conception, for rebirth of the soul's essence as it passes from stage to stage on its voyage back to God, the Mother Goddess that gives birth to enlightenment and *samadhi*—states of grace that manifest at the beginnings of time––when meditation practitioners embrace all of creation in the form of God's Beloved, the union of the human soul and the Universal Soul gives birth to a spiritual child who enters realms outside of time and space.

Creation always is. It doesn't stop because we're not conscious of its activity. It's not the job of the Mother Goddess to find her lost children. It's enough she gave birth to us. Her children have to find their way back to the point in time and space at the genesis of life. Her children have to learn to live in the moment. Her children have to become conscious of God's spectacle on Earth and in the cosmos. It's our work to form a covenant between kundalini and the Universal Soul, to become one with God and his beloved, the Mother Goddess who gives birth to creation.

Without that covenant, human beings are like herds of goats or sheep gone astray. They live in a material, emotional, and mental whirlpool of illusion that swirls and whirls around them like kaleidoscopic images from a dream. Their footing is very shaky. They've been divorced from the Mother Goddess, from their own higher being, from the moment, and from joy and love at the heart of all things.

What we're really trying to do through meditation practice is get real freedom. I don't mean freedom of religion, freedom of race, freedom from economic problems, and all these kinds of freedoms that exist on the Earth. I'm talking about the big leagues here, and the big leagues is freedom from ourselves.

When we free ourselves from ourselves and embrace the Mother Goddess, the union of our soul with the higher soul gives birth to an enlightened person. It's simply a process of evolution. We emerge from a dark, shadowlike crypt to the light of day. We become spiritual seekers that work hard to develop breath and mind and chakras because they're tools needed to get to God. We become spiritual seekers in quest of freedom. We no longer accept banal answers to profound questions. We no longer pride ourselves on intelligent maneuvering of karmic pieces on life's chessboard. We build our spiritual house a brick at a time, never forgetting the foundation is as important as the penthouse or game room. If we don't wire the house and put in plumbing, it's an impossible place in which to live. It's always smart to return to basics. The basics make it possible for us to continue on the path.

Name tags have little or nothing to do with enlightenment. The greatest saints never promote themselves or look for attention; the greatest teachers have no students. They've already given all their teachings away. They engage in dialogues with God, dialogues steeped in silence and in nothingness, wordless dialogues spoken from the heart, joyful dialogues, grateful dialogues, silence emanating from the womb of the Mother Goddess, silence touching on all of creation.

Seeing the Other Side of Ourselves

People often ask me where I learned the things I talk about. Since none of it seems extraordinary to me, it's hard to answer the question. I don't read books on meditation and spiritual practice. Before I started deep work on myself, I had no idea what any of this was about, but thirty years of meditation practice creates landscapes and perspectives. An inner life unfolds. We penetrate mysteries of a higher nature. We begin to see what's on the other side of ourselves.

Time passes, whether we like it or not. There's nothing we can do about it. But the thought of spending thirty years without deep meditation practice, the thought of growing old and thick and bored and filled with fear of the unknown, is enough to make me sit down and work deeply on myself. The years pass anyway, so one might as well do something intelligent with them.

T. S. Eliot, in *The Love Song of J. Alfred Prufrock* sang the following refrain: "I grow old/I grow old/I shall wear the bottoms of my trousers rolled" He went on to ask, "Do I dare to eat a peach?" The very thought is scary. It paralyzes the mindset of people. Most young, active, busy go-getters trip and fall over themselves when age sets in. When the inevitable happens, they barely have the strength to eat a peach. The wisdom of age is left behind in the frenzy of youth. As time passes, inner fire and passion extinguish themselves. We get old, ill, crippled, and afraid and can no longer hide from death. We wonder what happened, but the answer's simple. We took youth for granted and never, not for a moment, did we consider deep inner work an important life ingredient.

My particular meditation practice is not everyone's taste, but it works for me and for small groups of people around the world. It has never attracted great mobs. The work is difficult, and consistent, and its benefits come over long periods of time. There are no instant results. Like a good wine, the bouquet's a byproduct of years of patience. But in my heart, I believe there's a spiritual path for every human being. Be it meditation, art, music, religion, or dance, we all find our way through life. We all do exactly what we're born on Earth to do. Every human being is part of the Universal Soul. Every human being is given the gift of life and many opportunities to become one with higher creative energy in the universe.

Rudi lived and died in the thick of life. He believed all creativity existed in the unknown. He expanded his capacity as a human being, both in the world and on a transcendental level. He once visited me in Denton, Texas. We were standing on the porch of the ashram. He pointed to a small shopping center that bordered the ashram grounds. "I want you to buy that shopping center," he said. "But I've got only six hundred dollars in the bank," I said to him. "Anyone can do it with money," he replied with a big smile on his face. One month later, I bought the shopping center. Don't ask me how. I found vast resources of energy within myself and produced an economic miracle. Eventually, that shopping center made it possible for me to move back to New York City.

The struggle of a spiritual practitioner is alchemical. His tensions keep him down. His fear, insecurity, anger, and anxiety create a cesspool of pain. He must learn to transform tension into spirit, to free himself from himself so he can attain enlightenment. Problems never completely disappear, but they aren't necessarily unhealthy. They remind us we haven't arrived yet, that we haven't mastered every facet of life. They remind us we have to keep working on ourselves to transform our inner garbage into gold.

93683863R00132

Made in the USA
San Bernardino, CA
09 November 2018